A Narrative of
The Life of David Crockett
of the State of Tennessee

•TENNESSEANA EDITIONS•

A Narrative of
The Life of David Crockett
of the State of Tennessee
by David Crockett

A FACSIMILE EDITION WITH

ANNOTATIONS AND AN INTRODUCTION BY

James A. Shackford AND *Stanley J. Folmsbee*

KNOXVILLE  THE UNIVERSITY OF TENNESSEE PRESS

TENNESSEANA | TE EDITIONS

Nathalia Wright, General Editor

In the Tennessee Mountains by Mary Noailles Murfree (Charles Egbert Craddock), with an introduction by Nathalia Wright.

William G. Brownlow: Fighting Parson of the Southern Highlands by E. Merton Coulter, with an introduction by James W. Patton.

History of Middle Tennessee; or, Life and Times of Gen. James Robertson by A. W. Putnam, with an introduction by Stanley F. Horn and index by Hugh and Cornelia Walker. Published in cooperation with the Tennessee Historical Commission.

A Narrative of the Life of David Crockett of the State of Tennessee by David Crockett, a facsimile edition with annotations and an introduction by James Atkins Shackford and Stanley J. Folmsbee.

Frontispiece, David Crockett, courtesy of the State of Tennessee, Tourism Development Division.

Library of Congress Cataloging in Publication Data

Crockett, David, 1786–1836.
 A narrative of the life of David Crockett of
the State of Tennessee.

 (Tennesseana editions)
 Original ed. published in 1834 by E. L. Carey
and A. Hart, Philadelphia.
 1. Crockett, David, 1786–1836. 2. Tennessee—
History. 3. Creek War, 1813–1814. I. Shackford,
James Atkins, ed. II. Folmsbee, Stanley John,
1899–ed. III. Title. IV. Series.
F436.C9395   1973   976.8'04'0924 [B]
ISBN 0–87049–119–9   72–177358

Foreword

Among the notable folk heroes of this nation, David Crockett may well rank foremost in terms of the misconceptions and exaggerations of his life and exploits. Even before his death at the Alamo in 1836, the Davy Crockett legend was already building, and succeeding generations of writers and reprinters have more often than not confused rather than clarified the facts concerning Tennessee's famed Indian fighter, politician, and frontier humorist. Oddly enough, a major cause of the confusion has been his so-called "Autobiography," *A Narrative of the Life of David Crockett of the State of Tennessee* (Philadelphia: E. L. Carey and A. Hart; Baltimore: Carey, Hart and Co., 1834), at once myth-making and at the same time the most reliable source available for ascertaining the truth. Although this work is itself not completely reliable, the main corruption in the past has come from the inclusion with it, in a succession of reprints, of much spurious and extraneous material. For example, the best-known twentieth-century edition contains not only the original work, but also *An Account of Col. Crockett's Tour of the North and Down East* (mainly reprints of newspaper clippings, and published by the same company in 1835) and *Col. Crockett's Exploits and Adventures in Texas* (actually published in 1836 by Carey and Hart, but with the title page carrying the name of an apparently nonexistent firm: T. K. and P. G.

Collins, Philadelphia). All three of these accounts appeared in 1923 as the popular *Autobiography of David Crockett, with an Introduction by Hamlin Garland* (New York: Scribner's). The inclusion of *Texas Exploits* in this trilogy is particularly surprising. The reason for the subterfuge in regard to the imprint of the publisher is clearly indicated in a "Bibliographical Note" on page 11, which begins: "That *Col. Crockett's Exploits and Adventures in Texas* (1836) is spurious no one now seriously doubts." The note continues with a weak explanation of why it was decided to include this reprint anyway. The bibliographical notice, of course, received little attention, and practically everything written since 1923, as well as before, about David Crockett or the Alamo massacre is seriously distorted by major dependence on that counterfeit work.

The text portion of the present edition of the *Narrative* is a facsimile of the copy of the first edition held by the Tennessee State Library in Nashville. Text markers for the annotations have been superimposed upon the actual pages of this first edition. The annotations and the introduction for this new edition are based on those in a doctoral dissertation by the late James Atkins Shackford. His work, "The Autobiography of David Crockett, An Annotated Edition with Portraits, Maps, and Appendices" (2 vols., 730 pp.), was accepted by the faculty of the Graduate School of Vanderbilt University, Nashville, Tennessee, in 1948. Shackford considered his dissertation the first step in the preparation of a definitive biography of Crockett, and he subsequently prepared the manuscript for that book, but his illness and death prevented its submission to a publisher. His brother, John B. Shackford, then edited the work for publication in 1956 by the University of North Carolina Press under the title *David Crockett: The Man and the Legend.* This latter study remains, even today, the only authoritative work in book-length form on the life of the noted Tennessee frontiersman.

James Shackford, then, is co-editor of the present edition, both in recognition of his pioneering scholarship on this subject and because of my heavy reliance on his dissertation (as well as his biography) throughout this new rendering of the *Narrative.* In many instances, I have used Shackford's exact phraseology; in other cases, Shackford's research has been used, although it is presented in different language. Additionally, I have supplemented, and sometimes corrected, the information in both the dissertation and the biography.

Stanley J. Folmsbee
Professor Emeritus of History
The University of Tennessee

Contents

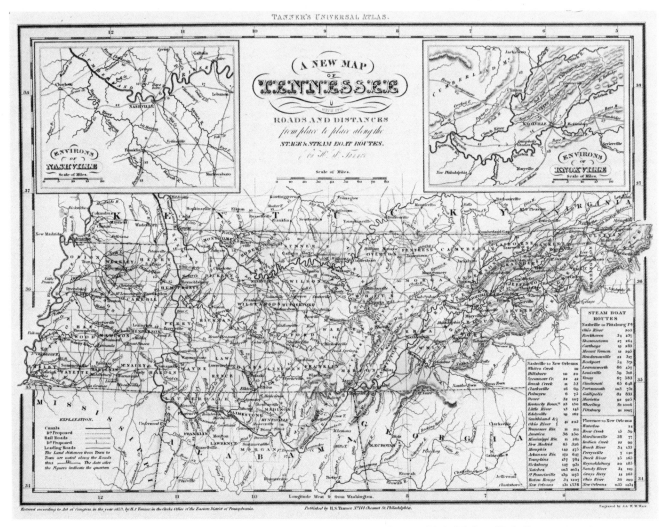

Crockett's Tennessee. Engraving by J. & W. W. Warr in TANNER'S UNIVERSAL ATLAS *(Philadelphia: H. S. Tanner, 1833).*

viii

Introduction TO THE NEW EDITION

A Narrative of the Life of David Crockett is an important document in three major areas of American culture. As a literary work, it is one of the earliest autobiographies to be published, only a decade and a half after the virtually complete version of the first of all, Benjamin Franklin's. Another American success story, it belongs in the long series of autobiographies telling similar stories, from Franklin to Malcolm X. It is also a very early extended example of American humor, the first of the Southwest variety, appearing just a year after Seba Smith's *Life and Writings of Major Jack Downing of Downingville* (Boston, 1833), the first example of the Yankee variety. It is, furthermore, a document of importance in the history of American English, being replete with dialectal usages, proverbial expressions, and spellings representing non-standard pronunciations. Crockett is credited, in fact, with being the first to use in print some half a dozen such locutions. His *Narrative* is, finally, a historical document. Because of the interest and background of the editors, this Introduction and the annotations of the text emphasize this aspect of the book.

There is presumably no written record of the exact month of publication of the *Narrative* or the exact number of printings since the book first appeared and before other titles were combined with it. Further, no date can be surmised from reviews or news stories by the press because the book apparently was not mentioned, although it was extremely popular with the readers of the time. There is some evidence, however, that the first edition was published in the early months of 1834. The Preface of the *Narrative* is dated February 1, 1834, and the copyright note indicates that the book was entered in the Clerk's Office of the District Court of the District of Columbia within that year. In addition, a series of advertisements bound in the back of the book itself carries the date "March 1834" preceding a list of books with the general heading, "New Works Lately Published, and Preparing for Publication, by E. L. Carey, and A. Hart, Philad. and Carey, Hart & Co. Baltimore, and For Sale by All Booksellers."

In regard to the number of printings of the original edition, there were at least seven reprints before spurious editions appeared because the Tennessee State Library holds a copy of the first printing and the University of Tennessee Library, Special Collections, in Knoxville houses a copy of the seventh edition, also dated 1834. The only difference between these two copies, aside from the edition notice, is the correction in the seventh edition of typographical errors found in the first edition. The Library of Congress' *The National Union Catalog Pre-1956 Imprints* lists, in addition to the original issue at Philadelphia and Baltimore, the following places of publication of reprints in 1834 for the *Narrative*: London (J. Limbird), Cincinnati (U. P. James), Boston (Allen & Ticknor), and Philadelphia (E. L. Carey & A. Hart).

Behind the myth represented by the popularized Davy Crockett stands an authentic folk hero, a man not as "supernatural" or extravagant as his mythical counterpart but nonetheless a fascinating figure. Here in the *Narrative* may be discovered the factual roots of the real David Crockett, the frontier humorist and teller of tall tales, the naïve yet wily mountaineer who feigned more ignorance than could be found in his makeup, the politician, the Indian fighter, and the rough-and-ready hero.

The myth of David Crockett was long evolving, and it is dying hard even yet. Although the scholarly investigating of James A. Shackford led to the publication of *Crockett* more than a decade and a half ago, numerous books about Crockett that preceded the Shackford volume remain in print, and hence school children and the public still hear more about the myth than the man. Crockett himself contributed to the myth-making during his lifetime, and it continued long after his death, experiencing a hearty revival as recently as the 1940s and 1950s. Aside from the tendency in the past for historians and scholars in literature to neglect the historical Crockett, the myth was given great impetus by the Walt Disney television program and motion picture, resulting in the widespread fad among children of wearing coonskin caps and singing about the "King of the Wild Frontier."[1]

At the base of the difficulty in separating the man from the legend have been the spurious and unreliable works that were added to most editions of the *Narrative*, beginning only three years after the book was first published. Even the *Narrative* itself, when unadorned by explication, is confusing and often misleading to the contemporary reader. Written for Crockett rather than by his own hand, it was politically inspired, leading to several intentional deviations from the truth (although the historical facts are generally quite accurate), as well as a number of unintentional errors, chiefly in the dating of events; additionally, the work is filled with historical allusions, which are quite difficult to appreciate unless the historical background and the political motivation are understood. Thus, by the time the largely fictitious *Texas Exploits* and the equally unreliable *Tour of the North* had been added to the *Narrative*, the real David Crockett and the myth were hopelessly intertwined. A succession of reprints, each including at least one of the spurious additions, continued to obscure the historical Crockett from scholars and the general public alike.

The growth of the Crockett legend reached a climax in the 1940s and 1950s, and it became a popular concept that the historical David Crockett was unknowable. Professor Walter Blair, for example, in an article, "Six Davy Crocketts,"[2] wrote off as unrecapturable "the Crockett God made" and also disregarded four other Crocketts, which he considered political creations essentially irreconcilable and unknowable. He concluded that the only

---

[1] One result of the song, according to a newspaper report, was an incident in Philadelphia when a group of school children were taken to Independence Hall to see the Liberty Bell. One child suddenly began to cry because the crack which Davy Crockett had supposedly fixed was still there! Even Estes Kefauver used a coonskin cap as a symbol when he was running for the Senate in 1948 and was being derided by the Memphis political boss Ed Crump. Charles Edmunson, "How Kefauver Beat Crump," *Harper's Magazine* 198 (Jan. 1949), 79–82.

[2] *Southwest Review* 25 (July 1940), 443–62.

Crockett of any importance was the Crockett myth.

Rather strangely, the students of American humor and folklore who so elevated the legendary Crockett passed over the several accounts purportedly written by him with silence or faint praise. On the other hand, the students of literature and history who had the least respect for Crockett, the man—such as V. L. Parrington, Russell Blankenship, and Charles A. Beard—have had the greatest respect for those accounts. For example, Parrington, deploring the lack of "authentic accounts of the frontier, written by men who had come out of it," stated:

> By far the most significant of them is the braggart but naïvely truthful narrative of the life of Cane-brake Davy .... As a full-length portrait of the Jacksonian leveler, ... [it] was the last pungent note of realism before the romantic revolution swept over American literature.[3]

In contrast, Franklin J. Meine in his *Tall Tales of the Southwest* [4] did not mention Crockett's *Narrative*, although he included an extract from the bastard *Texas Exploits*. Then he and Walter Blair in their anthology, *Mike Fink*,[5] set up Crockett as nothing but a myth by introducing him only in terms of legendary lore and the Crockett *Almanacs*, which had poured forth after his death. In 1939 Richard M. Dorson published a compilation of the *Almanacs*, with their fantastic tall tales, and in the "Foreword" to that work Howard M. Jones took the next step by claiming that the *Almanac* material was not merely a collection of yarns but was truly epic in its proportions.[6] Thus the need for a great American epic of the westward movement, proclaimed by Frank Norris in 1899,[7] seemed to have been fulfilled. In 1942 Richard Dorson declared: "The character of the legendary Crockett is similar in its evolution to the other heroes. Based on a striking personality, colored from ... frontier saga and enlarged through ... invention of many story-tellers, the fiction ... grew." [8] A year earlier Crockett had been highlighted in V. L. O. Chittick's *Ring-Tailed Roarers* [9] and described by Carl Van Doren in the Preface to E. J. Mayer's *Sunrise in My Pocket: The Last Days of Davy Crockett: An American Saga* [10] as being something of a Daniel Boone, Moses, and Prometheus. Finally, Irwin Shapiro, in 1944, contended that there had been "only one great epic figure in America, the figure of 'Davy' Crockett of the *Almanacs*." [11]

In his own book, *Yankee Thunder: The Legendary Life of Davy Crockett*,[12] Shapiro declared that any

> biographer of Davy Crockett is immediately confronted with a problem: which Davy Crockett shall he write about? For if there ever was a man of multiple identity, that man was Davy Crockett.

[3] *Main Currents in American Thought*, 3 vols. in 1 (New York, 1927), III, 390–91. For similar encomiums see Russell Blankenship, *American Literature* (New York, 1931), 225; Charles and Mary Beard, *The Rise of American Civilization*, 2 vols. in 1 (New York, 1941), 540.

[4] (New York, 1930.)

[5] (New York, 1933.)

[6] Dorson, ed., *Davy Crockett: American Comic Legend* (New York, 1939), xi–xiv.

[7] "A Neglected Epic," in *The Complete Works of Frank Norris* (New York, 1899), 279–82.

[8] "David Crockett and the Heroic Age," *Southern Folklore Quarterly* 6 (June 1942), 97.

[9] (Caldwell, Idaho, 1941.)

[10] (New York, 1941.)

[11] "An All-American Hero," *Saturday Review of Literature* 27 (Apr. 1, 1944), 10–11.

[12] (New York, 1944), p. 9.

First of all there was—or at least there exists some fairly reliable evidence to that effect—the flesh-and-blood Crockett, the frontiersman and hunter of early Tennessee. There was the historical Crockett, with his heroic exploits at the Alamo duly recorded in history. There was the political Crockett, a figure alternately built up and deflated by the Jacksonites and the anti-Jacksonites, according to the exigencies of the moment. And then there was the mythical Crockett, the Crockett of legend and folksay, of the tall tales and fireside yarns and almanac stories—the veritable yaller blossom of the forest, half horse, half alligator, with a little touch of snapping turtle, the ring-tailed roarer who could bring a coon out of a tree, ride a streak of lightning, wade the Mississippi, and come down off the Peak o'Day with a piece of sunrise in his pocket.

It was to this last Crockett, in the grand American tradition of Paul Bunyan, John Henry, Old Stormalong, and Pecos Bill, that I turned as being obviously the most credible, authentic, significant and true.

During that period nothing else which had the support of the historical scholar's name was written about Crockett. Meanwhile, throughout the nineteenth century and into the twentieth flowed a long stream of redactions of the *Narrative*, but with the spurious *Texas Exploits* and the *Tour of the North* added; the result was a practically worthless combination of legendary materials, anecdotes, errors, fictionalizings of one sort and another, along with a small amount of real history. There were some valuable reminiscences and a bit of valuable criticism, but the scholarship was sadly inaccurate and inadequate. As a result the historical Crockett was largely forgotten.

An understanding of the relative authenticity of the *Narrative* is best obtained by exploring how it came to be written and what its relationship is to an earlier version of Crockett's life, *The Life and Adventures of*

Colonel David Crockett of West Tennessee,[13] written by Mathew St. Clair Clarke, clerk of the House of Representatives. A detailed comparison of the two reveals so many similarities that one must have been based on the other. Both contain types of information which only Crockett could have given the ghost writer.[14] One big difference between the two works is that *Life and Adventures* contained more of the boisterous yarning, the legendary figure than did the *Narrative* and had handicapped rather than helped Crockett in his campaign for Congress in 1833.[15] Therefore, he repudiated it: "I don't know the author of the book" (in the Preface of the *Narrative*).

A few years earlier, in 1830, James Kirke Paulding had written a stage play, "The Lion of the West," whose chief character, Colonel Nimrod Wildfire, was at once associated with David Crockett, who actually stood up and took a bow when he saw the play in Washington. Crockett's association with "Wildfire" was to contribute

[13] (Cincinnati, 1833); the volume was reprinted later that year in New York and London as *Sketches and Eccentricities of Colonel David Crockett of West Tennessee*.

[14] For the conclusive evidence that Clarke was the ghost writer of *Life and Adventures* and not of the *Narrative*, see Shackford, *Crockett*, 258–64.

[15] After serving two terms in the Tennessee legislature, 1821–25, Crockett had run for Congress in 1825, but was defeated by Adam Alexander, whom he defeated for the post in 1827 and 1829. After his defeat in 1831, Crockett was elected again in 1833, defeating Fitzgerald, but was defeated in 1835 by Adam Huntsman. He then went to Texas and lost his life at the Alamo. The authors of at least one work on Crockett—Judge John Morrison and Col. Bob Hamsley, *The Real David Crockett* (Lawrenceburg, Tenn., 1955)—were unaware that before 1870 congressional as well as state elections in Tennessee were held

to his defeat for re-election to Congress in 1831 by William Fitzgerald. On December 4, 1830, the Jackson *Gazette* in his home district of West Tennessee had carried a letter comparing Fitzgerald to Crockett (or "Wildfire"):

> It is true, he [Fitzgerald] can't "whip his weight in wildcats," nor "leap the Mississippi," nor "mount a rainbow and slide off into eternity and back at pleasure . . . ." But this we believe, that Mr. Fitzgerald will make a better legislator; that he will as far excel Col. Crockett upon the floor of Congress as the Col. does him in the character of a mountebank . . . .

More important in explaining his defeat were Crockett's break with the Jacksonians on the issue of his Tennessee land bill (which they would not support) and his vote against the Indian removal bill of 1830. The chief cause of Crockett's break with Jackson, which happened during Crockett's first term rather than at the beginning of the second (as erroneously stated in Chapter XVII of the *Narrative*) was the land question. During his term in Congress in 1827 he first supported a measure introduced by his Tennessee colleague, James K. Polk, for the cession by the United States to Tennessee for educational purposes of all the remaining lands in the so-called "Congressional Reservation," which included all of Crockett's district of West Tennessee and the southwestern part of

Middle Tennessee. Becoming fearful that under Polk's bill the Tennessee legislature, of which he had been a member for two terms, would not adequately protect the rights of the "squatters" who had occupied much of the land before it could be offered for sale,[16] Crockett decided to introduce an alternative measure as an amendment. The efforts of the two Tennesseans during the second session of the Twentieth Congress to work out a compromise failed, and no Tennessee land bill was passed. Crockett naïvely accepted the support of anti-Jackson congressmen from the North in opposing the Polk bill, apparently expecting that after it was defeated, they would help him get his bill through. He seems not to have realized that his new "friends" were insincere, hoping to break up the Jackson party as well as to prevent any Tennessee land bill from passing. Nevertheless, Crockett became very angry at his Tennessee colleagues because they refused to shift their support from Polk's bill to his. Thus a major issue in his campaign for re-election in 1829 was the charge that he had deserted Jackson and joined the opposition. As early as January 16, 1829, Polk had written to a Tennessee friend, David McMillen,[17] attributing the defeat of his land bill and

in the odd-numbered instead of even-numbered years and incorrectly assumed that he was elected in 1826, 1828, 1832, and 1834. After being elected in August of the odd-numbered years, the Tennessee congressmen had plenty of time to get ready for the first regular session convening the following December. Fortunately, during Crockett's tenure no special sessions were called after the preceding Congress had gone out of existence on Mar. 3.

[16] Crockett also feared the money might be used for a college instead of common schools. When his son, John Wesley, was in Congress in 1841, a bill was passed permitting Tennessee to sell the lands on behalf of the U.S.; but John Wesley was not a member in 1846, when the act was passed actually ceding the lands (and the funds accrued under the act of 1841), to the state with a provision that $40,000 of the proceeds be used for the support of a college in West Tennessee. Henry D. Whitney, *The Land Laws of Tennessee* . . . (Chattanooga, 1891), 284–85, 301–303.

[17] Herbert Weaver and Paul H. Bergeron, *Correspondence of*

A letter from David Crockett. From the Tennessee Historical Society Miscellaneous Collection, courtesy of the State of Tennessee, Tourism Development Division.

of his effort to get some money for public education in the state

in a great degree to the course taken by our man *Crocket* [*sic*], who I regret to say opposed the very Bill at this Session, which he himself had agreed to in committee and supported and voted for in the House at the last session of Congress. He associated himself with our political enemies, and declared that he would vote for any measure any member wished him to vote for, providing he would vote for his foolish amendment and against the original bill.

That Crockett was shifting to the anti-Jackson side is indicated by his changing relationships with the anti-Jackson publishers of the *Register of Debates in Congress*, Joseph Gales and William Seaton. On February 5, 1828, during John Quincy Adams' administration, Crockett referred to Gales as a "treasury pap Sucking Editor." By April 18, 1829, he was writing Gales and Seaton a very friendly letter.[18] Actually, by February, a pro-Jackson congressman from Knoxville, Pryor Lea, was claiming that the publishers were writing David's speeches for him. Despite vigorous Jacksonite opposition, Crockett was re-elected in August 1829 and then

James K. Polk (2 vols. to date, Nashville, 1969–), I, 229–31. In Shackford, *Crockett*, the name is given incorrectly as Davison M. Millen.

[18] The Crockett letters are reproduced in the appendix of Shackford, "The Autobiography," 417–20, 433–35. For the Tennessee public land system, the Polk-Crockett controversy, and the violent denunciations of Crockett by other pro-Jackson congressmen from Tennessee, especially Pryor Lea of Knoxville (with whom he almost fought a duel) during his campaign for re-election in 1829, see Stanley J. Folmsbee and Anna Grace Catron, "David Crockett: Congressman," East Tennessee Historical Society's *Publications* 29 (1957), 43–58 (hereafter cited as ETHS *Publications*).

became more open in his opposition to Jackson. One example was his vote against Old Hickory's pet measure, the Indian removal bill passed May 24, 1830, appropriating $500,000 to provide for the removal of the Indians still living east of the Mississippi River to the western part of the Louisiana Purchase. Although the published *Register of Debates* does not have any reference to any Crockett speech on the removal bill, the Jackson *Gazette* [19] carried a summary of a Crockett speech of May 24, 1830, in which he denounced the measure, but admitted that he did not know anyone within five hundred miles of his home who would have voted the way he did. He believed the United States was bound by treaty to protect the Indians, and he would not vote to "remove them in the manner proposed."

Crockett came back and defeated Fitzgerald in the election of 1833, and the *Narrative*, published in 1834, was designed as a campaign document to help him win re-election in 1835. But it failed. The Jacksonites succeeded in getting Adam Huntsman, a "wheelhorse" of the party, to run against him, and Crockett was defeated.

He is reputed to have said that his constituents could go to Hell, and he would go to Texas.[20]

The *Narrative*, as clearly shown by Crockett's letters to his son, John Wesley, and to the publishers, Carey and Hart, was ghost-written by Thomas Chilton, a congressman from Kentucky. On January 10, 1834, he wrote to his son:

> I am ingaged in writing a history of my life and I have completed one hundred and ten pages and I have Mr Chlton [Chilton] to correct it as I write it [.] . . .
>
> I may take a trip through the eastern States during the recess of Congress and Sell the Book . . . a great many have preswaded me . . . that my presents [presence] will make thousands of people buy my book . . . .

In a letter of February 3, 1834,[21] accompanying the manuscript to Carey and Hart, he wrote: "It has been hastily passed over for correction . . . . It needs no correction of *spelling* or *grammar*, as I make no literary pretensions[.]" In a later letter, of February 23, again to

---

[19] (June 26, 1830); that issue was incorrectly dated on the masthead as June 19. Exactly the same summary, "A Sketch of the Remarks of the Hon. David Crockett . . ." was printed in *Speeches on the Passage of the Bill for the Removal of the Indians, Delivered in the Congress of the United States* (Boston, 1830), but the date of delivery was given as May 19. Incidentally, the Disney film depicted Crockett as rushing back to Washington from his tour of the North and East (1834) to tear in half and declaim against the Indian bill (passed in 1830). It is quite probable that Crockett made the speech but induced his friends Gales and Seaton to keep it out of the published *Debates*. They may have doublecrossed Crockett and released it as a part of their plan to build him up as an anti-Jacksonite of national proportions.

[20] Folmsbee and Catron, "Crockett: Congressman," 76–78; Shackford, *Crockett*, 195–211; Chase C. Mooney, "The Political Career of Adam Huntsman," *Tennessee Historical Quarterly* 10 (June 1951), 99–125; James D. Davis, *History of the City of Memphis* (1873; rpt. Memphis, 1972), 143. A letter Crockett wrote on the "eve of Starting" (Oct. 31, 1835) indicates that he had no intention then of joining the fight for Texan independence. Instead, his aim seems to have been to "explore" the country where he might want to settle. His last known letter— to Margaret (his daughter) and Wiley Flowers from St. Augustine, Jan. 9, 1836, describing his volunteering for service— repeats his desire to find a place to settle. This last letter is in the possession of J. D. Pate, Martin, Tenn.; a reproduction, made from a copy in the Univ. of Tennessee Library's Special Collections, is in Stanley J. Folmsbee and Anna Grace Catron, "David Crockett in Texas," ETHS *Publications* 30 (1958), 48–52.

[21] (Boston Public Library.)

Carey and Hart, however, he was somewhat more revealing:

> I wish you also to understand that the Hon Thos Chilton of Kentucky is entitled to one equl half of the Sixty two and a half *per cent* of the entire profits of the work as by the agreement between you and my Self—and also to half the Copy right in any Subsequent use . . . [.] The manuscript of the Book is in his hand writing though the entire Substance of it is truly my own . . . .

Crockett's agreement that the Kentuckian should receive one-half of the royalties and the fact that he told the publisher the manuscript was entirely in Chilton's handwriting indicate that the ghost-writer had much more than "passed over" to "correct it" as stated in the above letters. Although the work has many grammatical errors, they are not the same type of errors that Crockett made in his own correspondence. Chilton merely threw them in to supply flavor. Also, at Crockett's insistence, the tall-tale aspect which had characterized *Life and Adventures* was toned down. Nevertheless, the *Narrative* still includes (Chapter XIII) one interesting story about his method of campaigning: he carried a twist of tobacco as well as a bottle of liquor, so that he could leave the voter in as good shape as he found him.

Although the language of the *Narrative* is largely Chilton's, the information was supplied by Crockett, primarily by interviews but possibly also by a few notes which he may have written down. In addition, considerable use was made of *Life and Adventures*, for which Crockett had presumably supplied most of the information similarly to Clarke (the author of that work), despite his assertions to the contrary. A very careful comparison of the authentic records about Crockett with the autobiographical account of them reveals only two forms of discrepancies: first, a few additions and several seemingly deliberate alterations that may be attributed to Crockett's intention of having the *Narrative* serve partially as campaign literature for him; and second, errors not in stating fact but in supplying dates. The rest of the *Narrative*, however, is so meticulously accurate, as established by surviving records, that it proves conclusively that, in context, the work is all Crockett's—as he claimed it was. Thus, the guiding spirit, the realism, the humorous adventure, the historical fact, the rude but real heroism—these are largely Crockett's. Despite various expressions which seem to have emanated from Chilton, the general style, too, is Crockett's.

Among the intentional deviations from the truth, in addition to Crockett's disavowal of any connection with *Life and Adventures*, was his tendency to pose, like some current demagogues, as being much more ignorant than he really was to attract the votes of the poor, illiterate West Tennessee farmers. Some writers took him at his word and came to the conclusion that he was a nonentity, instead of recognizing his exaggeration. For example, his statements (in Chapter X) that when he ran for the legislature the first time he had never seen a public document and had never heard of the judiciary obviously were not true—a former squire, court referee, town commissioner, and a colonel commandant of the militia would be very familiar with both of them. Also, like other politicians, he was not always reliable in reporting election returns, especially when he was defeated. Even so, his report of the results of the 1831 election (Chapter XVII), that he had "a majority in seventeen counties, putting all their votes together, but the eighteenth [Madison] beat me," is technically correct. Counting only the votes of the "seventeen counties," leaving out Madison entirely, he would have had a margin of 586 votes over Fitzgerald.[22]

Another instance of unjustified questioning of Crockett's memory involves his statement in Chapter I of the *Narrative* that his mother, Rebecca Crockett, "was born in the state of Maryland, between York [Pennsylvania] and Baltimore." In 1928, Janie P. C. French and Zella Armstrong claimed in their genealogy [23] of the Crockett family that David's mother, Rebecca Hawkins, was a sister of Sarah Hawkins, the first wife of John Sevier. This would mean that she was born in the Shenandoah Valley of Virginia instead of in Maryland and that Crockett's statement is inaccurate. This view was generally accepted for many years except for the doubts privately expressed by another prominent genealogist, the late Mary Hoss Headman, a descendant of John and Sarah Hawkins Sevier.[24] After a careful investigation she became convinced that Sarah and Rebecca were not related, and that in many other respects the French and Armstrong genealogy is inaccurate, and so informed Stanley J. Folmsbee. The first challenge in print of the French and Armstrong theory was made in a little book, *Colonel*

"Davy" Crockett (Washington, D.C., 1956), by Robert M. Torrence and a collaborator, Robert L. Whittenburg (a Crockett descendant). They called attention to numerous errors in the French and Armstrong genealogy and reported that they had found in the records of St. Johns (later St. George) P. E. Church of Old Joppa, Maryland, located between Baltimore and York, Pennsylvania, at least two generations of the name Rebecca Hawkins. Also, there was a marriage record of a Joseph Hawkins to a Sarah MacDaniels, presumably of the same MacDaniels family known to have been neighbors of David Crockett's father and grandfather in Lincoln County, North Carolina, before they moved to the Tennessee country. The clinching argument, however, against the French and Armstrong thesis is one of ordinary common sense. If Crockett, born and raised in a region where the name of John Sevier was a household word, actually had been a nephew of the first governor of the state of Tennessee, he would have bragged about it in his *Narrative*.

The most significant deviations from fact in the *Narrative* are in Crockett's account of his participation in the Creek War. The records of his military service [25] prove conclusively that in his *Narrative* (Chapter VI) he distorted his account of his war record, probably for political purposes. For example, in his first enlistment Crockett volunteered for ninety days instead of sixty days as claimed in the book. The reason for the falsification

---

[22] Election returns, Archives Division, Tennessee State Library and Archives; Nashville *Republican and State Gazette,* Sept. 29, 1831. Samuel Cole Williams, *Beginnings of West Tennessee* (Johnson City, Tenn., 1930), misinterpreted Crockett's statement as saying he had a majority in each of the 17 counties. Actually, each candidate carried 9 of the 18 counties in the district.

[23] *The Crockett Family and Connecting Lines*, Vol. V of the Notable Southern Families Series (Bristol, Tenn., 1928), 328–29.

[24] Her genealogical records are in possession of her son, Francis W. Headman, Knoxville.

[25] Creek Indian War Muster and Payroll Records, War Records Division, National Archives. Photostatic copies of all those pertaining to the Tennessee troops are bound in unpaged volumes, under the title of "Records of the War of 1812," in Archives Division, Tennessee State Library and Archives.

was the desire to make it appear that when he allegedly participated, according to the *Narrative*, in a mutiny against Andrew Jackson, his term of service had already expired. According to Crockett's account, he was one of a group that marched boldly past a guard of soldiers Jackson had lined up to prevent their departure, and Crockett quoted Jackson as saying that they were "the damned'st volunteers he had ever seen in his life; that we would volunteer and go out and fight, and then at our pleasure would *volunteer* and go home again, in spite of the devil." This is somewhat similar to an event which actually occurred, but with this very important difference: Jackson seized a rifle, put it over the saddle of a horse, and threatened to shoot the first man who took another step toward home; the soldiers turned around and went back to their places. But Crockett was not a member of that group. Instead, he was one of General Coffee's mounted volunteers who were permitted to go home, recruit horses, get winter clothing, and rendezvous at Huntsville on December 8.[26] Crockett's prevarication was politically motivated; he apparently was attempting to justify his break with Jackson by claiming falsely that he had participated in a mutiny against him in the Creek War.

Crockett also claimed in the *Narrative* that he returned to service in December (which would have been an obvious impossibility had he actually been a mutineer) and agreed to serve another six months. Included in the *Narrative* are supposedly eyewitness accounts of two small engagements early in 1814 in which he did not partici-

pate—the accounts are based on histories of the Creek War available in 1834. Realizing that he could not take a chance on claiming he was at the big battle of Tohopeka (Horseshoe Bend) where the Creeks were crushed in March 1814, when he actually was not there, he gave himself a convenient furlough for that period of time. According to the official record of his service, he was discharged at the end of his first enlistment for ninety days on December 29, 1813, enlisted again on September 28, 1814, for six months, and was discharged on March 27, 1815. His own account of his service in 1814–15 (Chapters VII and VIII), however, seems to be authentic.[27]

Texas Exploits, on the other hand, is a prime example of dissimulation of facts. This book on Crockett's alleged Texas adventures has a history of misunderstanding and misinterpretation all its own. The original edition includes a Preface, signed by an Alex J. Dumas, which states that the manuscript was based on an "authentic" diary of David Crockett's which had been found on the battlefield of the Alamo and had been sent to Dumas by a Charles T. Beale to arrange for its publication. There is no evidence whatsoever that such a diary ever existed. Moreover, the names of both Dumas and Beale are fictitious, as are the names of the publishers, T. K. and P. G. Collins. The manuscript was written in its entirety in Philadelphia by Richard Penn Smith. That he was the author was revealed as early as 1839 in a sketch of him in *Gentleman's Magazine* [28] and was confirmed in 1842

---

[26] John Reid and John Henry Eaton, *Life of Andrew Jackson* (Philadelphia, 1817), 69–71, 90.

[27] To counterbalance the unfortunate dissimulations in ch. VI, it should be pointed out that the account does contain apparently valid information not available elsewhere, especially his story about the hungry soldiers eating potatoes.

[28] "Biography of Richard Penn Smith," *Gentleman's Maga-*

by Edgar Allan Poe in *Graham's Magazine*,[29] but it was not until 1884 that the real story came to light, with the publication in New York of J. S. Derby's reminiscence entitled *Fifty Years Among Authors, Books, and Publishers*. That work contains a very frank statement made to him by Mr. Hart, of Carey and Hart, which he recorded as follows:

> The late Richard Penn Smith was in Carey and Hart's one day, when Edward L. Carey told him that they had a large number of copies of Crockett's "Tour Down East" which didn't sell. Crockett had just been executed by the Mexican authorities at the Alamo, and Mr. Carey suggested to Mr. Smith, that if they could get up a book of Crockett's adventures in Texas, it would not only sell, but get them clear of the other books. They secured all the works on Texas they could lay their hands on, and Smith undertook the work. Mr. Carey said he wanted it done in great haste, and asked him when it would be ready for the printer; his reply was, "Tomorrow morning" [meaning obviously, early enough for a day's printing]. Smith came up to the contract, and never kept the printer waiting. The result was that a great many thousands of copies of the book were sold and all the balance of the edition of the "Tour Down East."[30]

That the Smith hoax was all too successful is quite evident. Despite Scribner's "Bibliographical Note" and the magazine articles of 1839 and 1842, prior to the appearance of Shackford's biography in 1956, practically everything published about David Crockett seems to have accepted the spurious *Texas Exploits* as genuine. Even a grandson of Crockett believed that an authentic diary had been found at the Alamo until Shackford disabused him. The grandson admitted, of course, that he had never seen the diary.[31] What is especially surprising is that the author of a Crockett biography, Constance Rourke,[32] made a slight beginning at writing from the sources, but then mixed fact and fiction so inextricably that her work is relatively useless. She expressed the opinion that the *Texas Exploits* might be genuine. Rourke attempted to discredit Derby's reminiscence by pointing out that it would have been impossible for Smith to write the entire book in one night—in other words by "tomorrow morning." She saw but refused to believe and thus ignored the obvious explanation in the sketch of Smith of 1839: "on the day succeeding that on which the idea was first suggested—a portion of this volume was actually in press and the remainder was supplied . . . so as to keep even pace with the stereotype founder." It is disillusioning, of course, to realize that the adventures of Crockett with the gambler and the bee hunter, especially as depicted by Disney in his movie, were figments of Richard Penn Smith's imagination.

Actually, the first two chapters of *Texas Exploits* do

---

zine, ed. W. E. Burton, V, 119–21. According to this sketch, he had "produced . . . 'Colonel Crockett's Tour of Texas,' a pseudo-autobiography . . . purported to have been written by the gallant Tennessean, prior to the fatal field of the Alamo"; also that "in the course of a single year upwards of ten thousand copies were sold," and it had been reprinted in London.

[29] "An Appendix of Autographs," *Graham's Magazine* 20 (Jan. 1842), 47. Poe listed among Smith's chief works: "a pseudo-auto-biography called 'Colonel Crockett's Tour in Texas.' " He also identified the author of the sketch in *Gentleman's Magazine* as a Mr. MacMichael, for whose judgment he had the "highest respect."

[30] As quoted in Shackford, *Crockett*, 274.

[31] *Ibid.*, 278.

[32] *Davy Crockett* (New York, 1934). See also her "Davy Crockett: Forgotten Facts and Legends," *Southern Review* 30 (Jan. 1934), 159.

have some validity; they seem to have been based on two letters sent by Crockett to Carey and Hart before he left for Texas. These chapters are the only ones in *Texas Exploits* (except for the final chapter) given as diary entries, and the dates are the same as the dates of the letters.[33] Although the first letter is not available, it is practically certain that a portion of the first chapter of *Texas Exploits* was based on it. The remainder summarizes from a recital in *Life and Adventures* one of Crockett's campaign stories—about using the "same identical" coonskin in getting ten quarts of liquor in a tavern for his crowd of listeners. The second chapter follows so closely the second letter that there can be no doubt about its use by Smith in the writing of that chapter. Thus the story of the discovery of a Crockett diary at the Alamo is proved fictitious.

Smith also was guilty of several mistakes that would not have been made by Crockett—for example, the misspelling of the name of Weakley County (see note 33), which is always spelled correctly in Crockett's correspondence. Early in Chapter III of *Texas Exploits* is the statement: "I . . . took hold of my rifle, Betsey, which all the world knows was presented to me by the patriotic citizens of Philadelphia . . . and thus equipped I started off [to Texas]." The evidence is conclusive that he did not take that rifle with him but left it at home. In the final chapter, in the entry dated February 23, there is a description of the flag flying over the Alamo: "it is composed of thirteen stripes, red and white, alternately, on a blue ground with a large white star, of five points, in the centre, and between the points the letters TEXAS." This is an excellent description of a flag which did not come into existence until some time *after* the Texas declaration of independence on March 2, 1836. The flag flying over the Alamo, February 23, as Crockett was well aware, was the Mexican constitution flag of 1824.[34]

Thus this fictitious account and the newspaper stories incorporated in the *Tour of the North* plus the famous *Life and Adventures* distort the historic picture of Crockett's life and the story of the Alamo. The only reliable source available for ascertaining the truth about David Crockett remains the *Narrative* itself. It is hoped that this new, annotated edition of that work will make both the book and its author more real, understandable, and appreciated. The *Narrative*, in our opinion, is a classic in American history as well as in American literature and in the American variety of English.

[33] The first letter, dated July 8, 1835, was advertised (according to Rourke, *Davy Crockett*, 268) in a catalog of John Heiss, Syracuse, N. Y., including a one-sentence extract: "I have great hope of writing one more book." The fourth paragraph (p. 2) of *Texas Exploits* starts: "I begin this book on the 8th day of July, 1835, at Home, Weakly [*sic*] county, Tennessee." The second letter, dated Aug. 11, 1835 (Maryland Historical Society), is somewhat similar to a letter to Gales and Seaton, dated Aug. 10, 1835, printed in *National Intelligencer*, Sept. 2, 1835.

[34] Shackford, *Crockett*, 280–81; Texas Jim Cooper, "A Study of Some David Crockett Firearms," ETHS *Publications* 38 (1966), 66–67.

A

NARRATIVE

OF THE

LIFE OF DAVID CROCKETT,

OF THE STATE OF TENNESSEE.

I leave this rule for others when I'm dead,
Be always sure you're right—THEN GO AHEAD!
THE AUTHOR.

WRITTEN BY HIMSELF

PHILADELPHIA:
E. L. CAREY AND A. HART.
BALTIMORE:
CAREY, HART & CO.

1834

PREFACE.

FASHION is a thing I care mighty little about, except when it happens to run just exactly according to my own notion ; and I was mighty nigh sending out my book without any preface at all, until a notion struck me, that perhaps it was necessary to explain a little the reason why and wherefore I had written it.

Most of authors seek fame, but I seek for justice,—a holier impulse than ever entered into the ambitious struggles of the votaries of that *fickle, flirting* goddess. [1]

A publication has been made to the world, which has done me much injustice; [2] and the catchpenny errors which it

3

1. Literary expressions of this type will occasionally be found throughout the volume ; these are probably phrases of Crockett's ghost-writer, Thomas Chilton.

2. The work referred to is, of course, *The Life and Adventures of Colonel David Crockett of West Tennessee* and its reissue in the same year under the title of *Sketches and Eccentricities of Colonel David Crockett of West Tennessee.*

3. We cannot accept Crockett's assertion that he did not know the author, or his statement in his letter of Jan. 17, 1834, to G. W. McLean: "I have no doubt but you have Sane [seen] a Book purporting to be the life and adventures of my Self[.] that book was written with out my knowledge and widely Circulated and in fact the person that took the first liberty to write the Book have published a Second addition [edition] and I thought one imposition was enough to put on the Country and I have put down the Imposition and have promised to give the people a Correct Statement of facts relative to my life. . . ." Library of Congress; hereafter cited as L. C. The author of *Life and Adventures* had to be known by Crockett, and Crockett further realized that the man behind the copyright name of James S. French was his old friend Mathew St. Clair Clarke, who surely received the information for *Life and Adventures* from Crockett.

4. Crockett continues to spoof, for now it is to his interest to tone down the tall tales he has so actively propagated about himself.

contains, have been already too long sanctioned by my silence. I don't know the author of the book—and indeed I don't want to know him; for after he has taken such a liberty with my name, and made such an effort to hold me up to public ridicule, he cannot calculate on any thing but my displeasure. If he had been content to have written his opinions about me, however contemptuous they might have been, I should have had less reason to complain.[3] But when he professes to give my narrative (as he often does) in my own language, and then puts into my mouth such language as would disgrace even an outlandish African, he must himself be sensible of the injustice he has done me, and the trick he has played off on the publick.[4] I have met with hundreds, if not with thousands of people, who have formed their opinions of my appearance, habits, language, and every thing else from that deceptive work.

They have almost in every instance expressed the most profound astonishment at finding me in human shape, and with the *countenance, appearance,* and *common feelings* of a human being. It is to correct all these false notions, and to do justice to myself, that I have written.

It is certain that the writer of the book alluded to has gathered up many imperfect scraps of information concerning me, as in parts of his work there is some little semblance of truth.[5] But I ask him, if this notice should ever reach his eye, how would he have liked it, if I had treated *him* so?—if I had put together such a bundle of ridiculous stuff, and headed it with *his* name, and sent it out upon the world without ever even condescending to ask *his* permission? To these questions, all upright

A 2

5. Unquestionably, there is more than "some little semblance of truth" in *Life and Adventures*, as contemporary records abundantly demonstrate.

men must give the same answer. It was
wrong; and the desire to make money
by it, is no apology for such injustice to a
fellow man.

But I let him pass; as my wish is greatly more to vindicate myself, than to con-
demn him.

In the following pages I have endeavoured to give the reader a plain, honest, home-
spun account of my state in life, and some
few of the difficulties which have attended
me along its journey, down to this time.
I am perfectly aware, that I have related
many small and, as I fear, uninteresting
circumstances; but if so, my apology is,
that it was rendered necessary by a desire
to link the different periods of my life together, as they have passed, from my childhood onward, and thereby to enable the
reader to select such parts of it as he may
relish most, if, indeed, there is any thing in
it which may suit his palate.

I have also been operated on by another consideration. It is this:—I know, that obscure as I am, my name is making considerable deal of fuss in the world. I can't tell why it is, nor in what it is to end. Go where I will, everybody seems anxious to get a peep at me ; and it would be hard to tell which would have the advantage, if I, and the " Government," and " Black Hawk,"[6] and a great eternal big caravan of *wild varments*[7] were all to be showed at the same time in four different parts of any of the big cities in the nation. I am not so sure that I shouldn't get the most custom of any of the crew. [8] There must therefore be something in me, or about me, that attracts attention, which is even mysterious to myself. I can't understand it, and I therefore put all the facts down, leaving the reader free to take his choice of them.

6. The "Government" was Andrew Jackson. "Black Hawk" was Adam Huntsman, the peg-legged lawyer who later defeated Crockett in the Aug. 1835 election.

7. *Varments* and *vermin* (and their variations in spelling) are used both figuratively and literally seven times in the *Narrative*. Crockett, on p. 58, applies the singular term to the girl who has jilted him.

8. This passage is apparently a slight reflection of an anecdote told at length in *Life and Adventures*. Many commentators take this and the next sentence literally, even though it is obviously meant to be humorous. V. L. Parrington, *Main Currents in American Thought*, II, 172–79, says such statements are indicative of Crockett's extreme and naïve egotism.

On the subject of my style, it is bad enough, in all conscience, to please critics, if that is what they are after. They are a sort of vermin, though, that I sha'n't even so much as stop to brush off. If they want to work on my book, just let them go ahead ; and after they are done, they had better blot out all their criticisms, than to know what opinion I would express of *them*, and by what sort of a curious name I would call *them*, if I was standing near them, and looking over their shoulders. They will, at most, have only their trouble for their pay. But I rather expect I shall have them on my side.

But I don't know of any thing in my book to be criticised on by honourable men.[9] Is it on my spelling ?—that's not my trade. Is it on my grammar ?—I hadn't time to learn it, and make no pretensions to it. Is it on the order and arrangement of my book ?—I never wrote one before, and never read very many; and, of course, know mighty little about that. Will it be on the authorship of the book ?—this I claim, and I 'll hang on to it, like a wax plaster. The whole book is my own, and every sentiment and sentence in it. I would not be such a fool, or knave either, as to deny that I have had it hastily run over by a friend or so, and that some little alterations have been made in the spelling and grammar; and I am not so sure that it is not the worse of even that, for I despise this way of spelling contrary to nature. And as for grammar, it's pretty much a thing of nothing at last, after all the fuss that's made about it. In some places, I wouldn't suffer either the spelling, or grammar, or any thing else to be touch'd; and therefore it will be found in my own way.

But if any body complains that I have

10. Shortly before Jackson removed the deposits from the Bank of the United States, he received (in June 1833) the honorary degree of doctor of laws from Harvard. The conferment angered his opponents, especially John Quincy Adams, who after that referred to him as "Doctor Andrew Jackson." John Spencer Bassett, *The Life of Andrew Jackson*, new ed., 2 vols. in 1 (New York, 1931), 638. Many passages in the *Narrative* reflect the influence of the pro-bank, anti-Jackson group who were using Crockett, with or without his fully realizing to what extent.

11. That members of the cabinet (especially Attorney General and acting Secretary of the Treasury Roger B. Taney) and the "kitchen cabinet" framed many official documents, and assisted in framing more, was widely known. This statement seems to be no less than a tacit admission that the authorship was not Crockett's in any literal sense. He does not say "no man *can* deny" but "no man *dares to deny*." It is as much as to say: "I wrote this book as Jackson wrote his proclamations—which all Jackson critics know (or at any rate, say) he didn't write." The humorous guise of the remark was meant to fool, and did fool, the readers; but it contained, nevertheless, the gist of truth.

12. Heel-tap: the small amount of liquor remaining in a glass after drinking.

had it looked over, I can only say to him, her, them—as the case may be—that while critics were learning grammar, and learning to spell, I, and "Doctor Jackson, L.L.D."[10] were fighting in the wars; and if our books, and messages, and proclamations, and cabinet writings, and so forth, and so on, should need a little looking over, and a little correcting of the spelling and the grammar to make them fit for use, its just nobody's business. Big men have more important matters to attend to than crossing their *t*'s—, and dotting their *i*'s—, and such like small things. But the "Government's" name is to the proclamation, and my name's to the book; and if I didn't write the book, the "Government" didn't write the proclamation, which no man *dares to deny!* [11]

But just read for yourself, and my ears for a heel tap,[12] if before you get through you don't say, with many a good-natured smile and hearty laugh, "This is truly the very thing itself—the exact image of its Author,

DAVID CROCKETT."

WASHINGTON CITY,
February 1st, 1834.

NARRATIVE

OF THE

LIFE OF DAVID CROCKETT.

CHAPTER I.

As the public seem to feel some interest in the history of an individual so humble as I am, and as that history can be so well known to no person living as to myself, I have, after so long a time, and under many pressing solicitations from my friends and acquaintances, at last determined to put my own hand to it, and lay before the world a narrative on which they may at least rely as being true. And seeking no ornament or colouring for a plain, simple tale of truth, I throw aside all hypocritical and fawning apologies, and, according to my own maxim, just *"go ahead."*[1] Where I am not known, I might, perhaps, gain some little credit by having thrown around this volume some of the flowers of learning; but

B   13

1. This motto has been widely publicized and interpreted, but perhaps a contemporary of Crockett takes the sanest position: "Three maxims creditable to their [the pioneers'] good sense, and practical bent, were rife among them; viz., 'Never judge a tree by the bark'; 'Never sneeze because somebody else has taken snuff'; 'Be sure you are right, then go ahead.' This last maxim is attributed as originally Crockett's. Doubtless he often heard it in his childhood and adopted it." S. H. Stout, "David Crockett," *American Historical Magazine* 7 (Jan. 1902), 14 (hereafter cited as *AHM*). "Go ahead" and its variations (e.g., "pushed ahead," "pursue on") occurs 42 times in the *Narrative* (first use, p. 8), but appears only once (as "go ahead") in the Crockett letters—to A. M. Hughes, Dec. 8, 1833 (Tennessee Historical Society, hereafter cited as THS).

2. Crockett alluded to a version of one of Aesop's fables: a jackdaw collected the fallen feathers of many beautiful birds to bedeck himself for a contest in which Jupiter would select the most beautiful bird to be king. The other birds, angry when Jupiter proposed making the jackdaw king, each reclaimed its own feathers, and "the Jackdaw was again nothing but a Jackdaw."

3. It probably was his grandfather, also named David, who was born at the time of the migration. Robert Crockett, one of his father's brothers, stated in his 1833 application for a Revolutionary War pension that he was born Aug. 13, 1755, at the site of Berryville, Va. Stanley J. Folmsbee and Anna Grace Catron, "The Early Career of David Crockett," ETHS *Publications* 28 (1956), 58–59. Very dubious are the contentions of Janie P. C. French and Zella Armstrong in *Davy Crockett and the Crockett Family* (Chattanooga, n. d.) and in *Crockett Family and Connecting Lines* (203–204) that David's great-grandfather William was born in 1709 in New Rochelle, N. Y., shortly after his father, Joseph, had come to America from Ireland, the date of which was given elsewhere in the book as about 1715–17! It is inconceivable that Crockett in the *Narrative* could have confused his father with his great-grandfather and that David's lineage goes back to Antoine de Crocketagne of 17th-century France. It is true, however, that the Crocketts were Scotch-Irish. Dr. Stout, "David Crockett," 18, recorded his boyhood recollection of meeting David in a Presbyterian church in Nashville in the pew of a relative, George Crockett, who said that both he and David were Scotch-Irish "decendants of the clan of Crocketts of the old country."

where I am known, the vile cheatery would soon be detected, and like the foolish jackdaw, that with a *borrowed* tail attempted to play the peacock, I should be justly robbed of my pilfered ornaments, and sent forth to strut without a tail for the balance of my time.[2] I shall commence my book with what little I have learned of the history of my father, as all *great men* rest many, if not most, of their hopes on their noble ancestry. Mine was poor, but I hope honest, and even that is as much as many a man can say. But to my subject.

My father's name was John Crockett, and he was of Irish descent. He was either born in Ireland or on a passage from that country to America across the Atlantic.[3] He was by profession a farmer, and spent the early part of his life in the state of Pennsylvania. The name of my mother was Rebecca Hawkins. She was an American woman, born in the state of Maryland, between York and Baltimore. It is likely I may have heard where they were married, but if so, I have forgotten. It is, however, certain that they were, or else the public would never have been troubled with the history of David Crockett, their son.

I have an imperfect recollection of the part which I have understood my father took in the revolutionary war.[4] I personally know nothing about it, for it happened to be a little before my day ; but from himself, and many others who were well acquainted with its troubles and afflictions, I have learned that he was a soldier in the revolutionary war, and took part in that bloody struggle. He fought, according to my information, in the battle at Kings Mountain[5] against the British and tories, and in some other engagements of which my remembrance is too imperfect to enable me to speak with any certainty. At some time, though I cannot say certainly when, my father, as I have understood, lived in Lincoln county, in the state of North Carolina. How long, I don't know. But when he removed from there, he settled in that district of country which is now embraced in the east division of Tennessee, though it was not then erected into a state.[6]

He settled there under dangerous circumstances, both to himself and his family, as the country was full of Indians, who were at that time very troublesome. By the Creeks, my grandfather and grandmother Crockett were both murdered,[7] in their own house, and on the very spot of ground where Rogersville, in Hawkins county, now stands.[8] At the same time, the Indians wounded Joseph Crockett, a brother to my father, by a ball, which

4. By 1776 the family of grandfather David had moved from Lincoln County, N. C., to the Holston-Watauga valleys, for the names of David and William Crockett were signed to the Washington District petition of July 5, 1776, and the names of John, William, and David (twice) were signed to petitions of 1776 and 1777 of Carter's Valley settlers to Virginia. Folmsbee and Catron, "Early Career," 59–60; J. G. Folmsbee and Catron, "Early Career," 59–60; J. G. M. M. Ramsey, *Annals of Tennessee* (Charleston, S. C., 1853; rpt. Knoxville, 1967), 138.

5. *Roster of Soldiers from North Carolina in the American Revolution* (Baltimore, 1967), 480, lists John Crockett as a member of the Lincoln County militia; Louise W. Reynolds states in "The Pioneer Crockett Family of Tennessee," *Daughters of the American Revolution Magazine* 55 (Apr. 1921), 188, that he served as a frontier ranger during the war but "returned to Washington County in time to participate" in the march over the mountains to fight in this battle.

6. On Dec. 29, 1789, the area of the present state of Tennessee was ceded by North Carolina to the federal government, and in 1790 the region was organized as the Territory South of the River Ohio. The new state of Tennessee was admitted on June 1, 1796.

7. The raid was made in the spring of 1777 (while John Crockett was away serving as a ranger) by Creeks and Chickamaugas (seceders from the Cherokees).

8. This county was formed from Sullivan County in 1786. A. P. Foster, *Counties of Tennessee* (Nashville, 1923), 21. Hawkins County records (Deed Book No. 1, p. 58; Circuit Court Minutes, 1810–21, pp. 58, 84 *passim*) show that the son of David's grandfather, one of David's uncles, sold his North Carolina Land

Grant No. 271 to Joseph Rogers, founder of Rogersville, on June 7, 1790. Typed copies of many Tennessee county records, including these deed books and court minutes, made by the WPA Historical Records Survey, are available in many libraries. A monument commemorating the massacre and the death of David's grandparents was erected in 1927 in Rogersville. Robert M. McBride, "David Crockett and His Memorials in Tennessee," *Tennessee Historical Quarterly* 26 (Fall 1967), 232; rpt. in his *More Landmarks of Tennessee History* (Nashville, 1969), 90 (hereafter page citations will be to the reprint).

9. There are numerous records of both men. A comment on the capture of James is in Sam K. Cowan, *Sergeant York and His People* (New York, 1922), 101: "It was in a house on the land now owned by Coonrod Pile that 'Deaf and Dumb Jimmy Crockett' spent the last years of his life, and from which he made so many journeys to locate the silver mine of the Indians who had held him captive . . . while they dug the silver ore . . . . David Crockett in his autobiography tells the story of 'Deaf and Dumb Jimmy' but he places the scene in Kentucky . . . ." On June 2, 1828, James Crockett sold to Conrod Pile a tract of land for $200 "below the three forks of Wolf River." Fentress County Deed Books, A, p. 362 (copied by WPA).

10. Actually, in 1834 it was Fentress County, Tenn. (created in 1823 from Overton and Morgan counties; Foster, *Counties*, p. 57). When Crockett presumably visited that area in 1816 or 1817 (before the Tennessee-Kentucky boundary dispute was settled in 1819), a six-mile-wide stretch of land south of the present line was claimed by Kentucky, which considered it a part of Cumberland County. For evidence that he actually lived there, see Albert R. Hogue, *David Crockett and Others in Fentress County* (Jamestown, Tenn., 1955), *passim*.

11. "Seventh" is perhaps a Biblical allusion; the

broke his arm ; and took James a prisoner, who was still a younger brother than Joseph, and who, from natural defects, was less able to make his escape, as he was both deaf and dumb.[9] He remained with them for seventeen years and nine months, when he was discovered and recollected by my father and his eldest brother, William Crockett ; and was purchased by them from an Indian trader, at a price which I do not now remember ; but so it was, that he was delivered up to them, and they returned him to his relatives. He now lives in Cumberland county, in the state of Kentucky;[10] though I have not seen him for many years.

My father and mother had six sons and three daughters. I was the fifth son. What a pity I hadn't been the seventh ! For then I might have been, by *common consent*, called *doctor*, as a heap of people get to be great men.[11] But, like many of them, I stood no chance to become great in any other way than by accident. As my father was very poor, and living as he did *far back in the back woods*, he had neither the means nor the opportunity to give me, or any of the rest of his children, any learning.

But before I get on the subject of my own troubles, and a great many very funny things that have happened to me, like all other historians and booagraphers, I should not only inform the public that I was born, myself, as well as other folks, but that this important event took place, according to the best information I have received on the subject, on the 17th of August, in the year 1786; whether by day or night, I believe I never heard, but if I did I, have forgotten. I suppose, however, it is not very material to my present purpose, nor to the world, as the more important fact is well attested, that I was born ; and, indeed, it might be inferred, from my present size and appearance, that I was pretty *well born*, though I have never yet attached myself to that numerous and worthy society.[12]

At that time my father lived at the mouth of Lime Stone, on the Nola-chucky river;[13] and for the purpose not only of showing what sort of a man I now am, but also to show how soon I began to be a *sort of a little man*, I have endeavoured to take the *back track* of life, in order to fix on the first thing that I can remember. But even then, as now, so many things were happening, that as Major Jack Downing would say, they are all in " a pretty considerable of a snarl," and I find it " kinder hard" to fix on that thing, among them all, which really happened first.[14] But I think it

number seven, found repeatedly in the Scriptures, is the number of Divine perfection. The reference to *doctor* is certainly to Andrew Jackson and his honorary degree, and although Jackson was a third son, not a seventh, he was the seventh President of the United States (1829–37).

12. No records of his birth date are extant, but Aug. 17 is probably correct.

13. Crockett has written that he was born at the mouth of Limestone Creek on the Nolichucky River. Rhea's Map of 1832 (rpt. Robert M. McBride and Owen Meredith, eds., *Eastin Morris' Tennessee Gazeteer, 1834, and Matthew Rhea's Map of the State of Tennessee, 1832* [Nashville, 1971]) shows "Big Limestone," emptying into the Nolichucky in Greene County near its eastern border, and "Lit. Limestone" a short distance east in Washington County. A marble slab now marks the presumed birthplace, on the north bank of Big Limestone. The site, owned by the Davy Crockett Birthplace Assoc., also includes a replica of the cabin and a visitors' center. McBride, "Crockett Memorials," 90–91.

14. Crockett here is taking advantage of the popularity of the Downing letters written by Seba Smith. The letters first appeared serially in newspapers, beginning on January 18, 1830, and then in book form. In a second series, *Downing Gazette*, beginning July 4, 1834, Smith, through Major Downing, turned violently away from Jackson, as Crockett had done previously. This series was omitted from his *My Thirty Years Out of the Senate. By Major Jack Downing* (New York, 1859). Shackford, *Crockett*, 196–97. Although Seba Smith's works were published as letters, in tone and character they had many qualities in common with the *Narrative*.

likely, I have hit on the outside line of my recollection ; as one thing happened at which I was so
badly scared, that it seems to me I could not have
forgotten it, if it had happened a little time only
after I was born.   Therefore it furnishes me with
no certain evidence of my age at the time ; but I
know one thing very well, and that is, that when
it happened, I had no knowledge of the use of
breeches, for I had never had any nor worn any.

But the circumstance was this : My four elder
brothers, and a well-grown boy of about fifteen
years old, by the name of Campbell, and myself,
were all playing on the river's side ; when all the
rest of them got into my father's canoe, and put
out to amuse themselves on the water, leaving me
on the shore alone.

Just a little distance below them, there was a
fall in the river, which went slap-right straight
down.   My brothers, though they were little fellows, had been used to paddling the canoe, and
could have carried it safely anywhere about there ;
but this fellow Campbell wouldn't let them
have the paddle, but, fool like, undertook to ma-
nage it himself.   I reckon he had never seen a
water craft before ; and it went just any way but
the way he wanted it.   There he paddled, and
paddled, and paddled—all the while going wrong,

—until, in a short time, here they were all going, straight forward, stern foremost, right plump to the falls ; and if they had only had a fair shake, they would have gone over as slick as a whistle. It was'ent this, though, that scared me ; for I was so infernal mad that they had left me on the shore, that I had as soon have seen them all go over the falls a bit, as any other way. But their danger was seen by a man by the name of Kendall, but I'll be shot if it was Amos ;[15] for I believe I would know him yet if I was to see him. This man Kendall was working in a field on the bank, and knowing there was no time to lose, he started full tilt, and here he come like a cane brake afire ; and as he ran, he threw off his coat, and then his jacket, and then his shirt, for I know when he got to the water he had nothing on but his breeches. But seeing him in such a hurry, and tearing off his clothes as he went, I had no doubt but that the devil or something else was after him—and close on him, too—as he was running within an inch of his life. This alarmed me, and I screamed out like a young painter.[16] But Kendall didn't stop for this. He went ahead with all might, and as full bent on saving the boys, as Amos was on moving the deposites.[17] When he came to the water he plunged in, and where it was too deep to

15. There are many names which cannot be identified, and others are purposely fabricated. For instance, "a man by the name of Kendall" is probably fictitious, created to take a dig at Jackson; Amos Kendall was one of Jackson's confidential circle of friends as well as postmaster general.

16. *Painter* for *panther* (or a bobcat or mountain lion) is still used in the eastern Tennessee and western North Carolina mountains.

17. *Deposites*, always spelled thus by the Whig publishers, Gales and Seaton, appears nine times in the *Narrative*, but in three letters written during the same period Crockett omits the second *e*. The removal of the government deposits from the Bank of the United States, which Kendall favored, was a part of Jackson's "War" against the Bank.

wade he would swim, and where it was shallow enough he went bolting on ; and by such exertion as I never saw at any other time in my life, he reached the canoe, when it was within twenty or thirty feet of the falls ; and so great was the suck, and so swift the current, that poor Kendall had a hard time of it to stop them at last, as Amos will to stop the mouths of the people about his stockjobbing. But he hung on to the canoe, till he got it stop'd, and then draw'd it out of danger. When they got out, I found the boys were more scared than I had been, and the only thing that comforted me was, the belief that it was a punishment on them for leaving me on shore.

Shortly after this, my father removed, and settled in the same county, about ten miles above Greenville.[18]

There another circumstance happened, which made a lasting impression on my memory, though I was but a small child. Joseph Hawkins, who was a brother to my mother, was in the woods hunting for deer. He was passing near a thicket of brush, in which one of our neighbours was gathering some grapes, as it was in the fall of the year, and the grape season. The body of the man was hid by the brush,

18. Crockett's use of the phrase "same county . . . above Greenville [Greeneville]" supports local tradition that the county of his birth was Greene. That his father was there in 1786, the year of David's birth, is shown by Greene County Court Minutes, 1783–96 (copied by WPA) for the Feb. 1786 term, pp. 47, 50, 52, listing John Crockett as a juryman and as a constable. Ten years later a "John Crockett" was tried on a charge of "petit larceny" but was acquitted. *Ibid.*, 468. At that time, however, David's father was living in Jefferson County.

and it was only as he would raise his hand to
pull the bunches, that any part of him could be
seen. It was a likely place for deer ; and my
uncle, having no suspicion that it was any human
being, but supposing the raising of the hand to
be the occasional twitch of a deer's ear, fired at
the lump, and as the devil would have it, unfortunately shot the man through the body. I
saw my father draw a silk handkerchief through
the bullet hole, and entirely through his body ;
yet after a while he got well, as little as any one
would have thought it. What become of him,
or whether he is dead or alive, I don't know ;
but I reckon he did'ent fancy the business of gathering grapes in an out-of-the-way thicket soon
again.

The next move my father made was to the
mouth of Core creek,[19] where he and a man by the
name of Thomas Galbreath undertook to build a
mill in partnership. They went on very well
with their work until it was nigh done, when
there came the second epistle to Noah's fresh,[20] and
away went their mill, shot, lock, and barrel. I
remember the water rose so high, that it got up
into the house we lived in, and my father moved
us out of it, to keep us from being drowned. I
was now about seven or eight years old, and have

19. Later editions of the *Narrative* corrected *Core*
to *Cove;* the original typesetter probably misread
Chilton's *v* as *r*. According to Reynolds, "Pioneer
Crockett Family," 189, "records extant show that in
1794, Thomas Galbreath received a permit to build a
mill upon that stream," but the Greene County Court
Minutes (p. 335) for the May 1794 term merely refer
to a "Thos. Galbreath Mill" as being located on the
road from Greeneville.

20. "Noah's fresh" is a reference to the Biblical
deluge. The site is now covered by Crockett Lake,
created by a dam built by TVA.

21. This county was formed by Territorial Governor William Blount on June 11, 1792, from parts of Greene and Hawkins counties. Foster, *Counties,* 22–23.

22. Abingdon, Va., to Knoxville. The land on which the tavern stood may have been later included in the 300 acres "on the South side of the Main Holston road and within a few miles of Perkinses Iron Works on Mossy Creek . . ." sold under the sheriff's hammer Nov. 4, 1795 (Jefferson County Deed Book Q, 94–95, as quoted in Shackford, *Crockett,* 6). Since John Crockett lost title to this land, near Jefferson City, it is more likely that the tavern was built where a replica of it was constructed in 1959 by the Hamblen County Chapter of the Association for the Preservation of Tennessee Antiquities, in Morristown. During an earlier excavation at the site in 1949, the remains of a mill lined with hand-hewn cedar were found at the exact spot where an old resident claimed the Crockett Tavern stood. Morristown *Daily Gazette and Mail,* July 21, 1949. However, according to Maxine Mathews, "Old Inns of East Tennessee," ETHS *Publications* 2 (1930), 31, John Crockett built his tavern eight miles east of Dandridge. Nevertheless, the Morristown site has been designated as an "official historic site" and identified by a Tennessee Historical Commission marker. McBride, "Crockett Memorials," 91–92. Incidentally, a nearby height of land has long been known as "Crockett's Ridge."

23. Here, but even more so in *Life and Adventures,* the Dutch are frequently mentioned. Probably the source of these references was Mathew Clarke, the author of *Life and Adventures,* who came from the Pennsylvania Dutch region of Pennsylvania.

a pretty distinct recollection of every thing that was going on. From his bad luck in that business, and being ready to wash out from mill building, my father again removed, and this time settled in Jefferson county,[21] now in the state of Tennessee; where he opened a tavern on the road from Abbingdon to Knoxville.[22]

His tavern was on a small scale, as he was poor; and the principal accommodations which he kept, were for the waggoners who travelled the road. Here I remained with him until I was twelve years old; and about that time, you may guess, if you belong to Yankee land, or reckon, if like me you belong to the back-woods, that I began to make up my acquaintance with hard times, and a plenty of them.

An old Dutchman,[23] by the name of Jacob Siler, who was moving from Knox county to Rockbridge, in the state of Virginia, in passing, made a stop at my father's house. He had a large stock of cattle, that he was carrying on with him; and I suppose made some proposition to my father to hire some one to assist him.

Being hard run every way, and having no thought, as I believe, that I was cut out for a Congressman or the like, young as I was, and as little as I knew about travelling, or being from

home, he hired me to the old Dutchman, to go
four hundred miles on foot, with a perfect stranger
that I never had seen until the evening before. I
set out with a heavy heart, it is true, but I went
ahead, until we arrived at the place, which was
three miles from what is called the Natural Bridge,
and made a stop at the house of a Mr. Hartley,
who was father-in-law to Mr. Siler, who had
hired me. My Dutch master was very kind to
me, and gave me five or six dollars, being pleased,
as he said, with my services.

This, however, I think was a bait for me, as he
persuaded me to stay with him, and not return
any more to my father. I had been taught so
many lessons of obedience by my father, that I
at first supposed I was bound to obey this man,
or at least I was afraid openly to disobey him ; and
I therefore staid with him, and tried to put on a
look of perfect contentment until I got the family
all to believe I was fully satisfied. I had been
there about four or five weeks, when one day myself and two other boys were playing on the road-
side, some distance from the house. There came
along three waggoners. One belonged to an old
man by the name of Dunn, and the others to two
of his sons. They had each of them a good team,
and were all bound for Knoxville. They had been

in the habit of stopping at my father's as they passed the road, and I knew them. I made myself known to the old gentleman, and informed him of my situation; I expressed a wish to get back to my father and mother, if they could fix any plan for me to do so. They told me that they would stay that night at a tavern seven miles from there, and that if I could get to them before day the next morning, they would take me home; and if I was pursued, they would protect me. This was a Sunday evening; I went back to the good old Dutchman's house, and as good fortune would have it, he and the family were out on a visit. I gathered my clothes, and what little money I had, and put them all together under the head of my bed. I went to bed early that night, but sleep seemed to be a stranger to me. For though I was a wild boy, yet I dearly loved my father and mother, and their images appeared to be so deeply fixed in my mind, that I could not sleep for thinking of them. And then the fear that when I should attempt to go out, I should be discovered and called to a halt, filled me with anxiety; and between my childish love of home, on the one hand, and the fears of which I have spoken, on the other, I felt mighty queer.

But so it was, about three hours before day in

the morning I got up to make my start.   When I
got out, I found it was snowing fast, and that the
snow was then on the ground about eight inches
deep.   I had not even the advantage of moonlight,
and the whole sky was hid by the falling snow,
so that I had to guess at my way to the big road,
which was about a half mile from the house.
I however pushed ahead and soon got to it, and
then pursued it, in the direction to the waggons.

I could not have pursued the road if I had not
guided myself by the opening it made between
the timber, as the snow was too deep to leave any
part of it to be known by either seeing or feeling.

Before I overtook the waggons, the earth was
covered about as deep as my knees ; and my
tracks filled so briskly after me, that by daylight,
my Dutch master could have seen no trace which
I left.

I got to the place about an hour before day.[24] I
found the waggoners already stirring, and engaged
in feeding and preparing their horses for a start.
Mr. Dunn took me in and treated me with great
kindness.   My heart was more deeply impressed
by meeting with such a friend, and " at such a
time," than by wading the snow-storm by night,
or all the other sufferings which my mind had
endured.   I warmed myself by the fire, for I was

C

24. Therefore, Crockett, at the age of 12, walked
seven miles in two hours in snow varying from eight
inches to knee-deep.

very cold, and after an early breakfast, we set out on our journey. The thoughts of home now began to take the entire possession of my mind, and I almost numbered the sluggish turns of the wheels, and much more certainly the miles of our travel, which appeared to me to count mighty slow. I continued with my kind protectors, until we got to the house of a Mr. John Cole, on Roanoke, when my impatience became so great, that I determined to set out on foot and go ahead by myself, as I could travel twice as fast in that way as the waggons could.

Mr. Dunn seemed very sorry to part with me, and used many arguments to prevent me from leaving him. But home, poor as it was, again rushed on my memory, and it seemed ten times as dear to me as it ever had before. The reason was, that my parents were there, and all that I had been accustomed to in the hours of childhood and infancy was there ; and there my anxious little heart panted also to be. We remained at Mr. Coles that night, and early in the morning I felt that I couldn't stay ; so, taking leave of my friends the waggoners, I went forward on foot, until I was fortunately overtaken by a gentleman, who was returning from market, to which he had been with a drove of horses. He had a led horse, with a bridle and saddle on him, and he kindly offered to let me get on his horse and ride him. I did so, and was glad of the chance, for I was tired, and was, moreover, near the first crossing of Roanoke, which I would have been compelled to wade, cold as the water was, if I had not fortunately met this good man. I travelled with him in this way, without any thing turning up worth recording, until we got within fifteen miles of my father's house. There we parted, and he went on to Kentucky[25] and I trudged on homeward, which place I reached that evening. The name of this kind gentleman I have entirely forgotten, and I am sorry for it ; for it deserves a high place in my little book. A remembrance of his kindness to a little straggling boy, and a stranger to him, has however a resting place in my heart, and there it will remain as long as I live.

25. Maps of 1795 show that the present route from Morristown to Middlesboro, through the Cumberland Gap, or one approximating the same route, was then in existence.

CHAPTER II.

Having gotten home, as I have just related, I remained with my father until the next fall,[1] at which time he took it into his head to send me to a little country school, which was kept in the neighbourhood by a man whose name was Benjamin Kitchen ; though I believe he was no way connected with the cabinet. [2] I went four days, and had just began to learn my letters a little, when I had an unfortunate falling out with one of the scholars,—a boy much larger and older than myself. I knew well enough that though the school-house might do for a still hunt, it wouldn't do for *a drive*, and so I concluded to wait until I could get him out, and then I was determined to give him salt and vinegar. I waited till in the evening, and when the larger scholars were spelling, I slip'd out, and going some distance along his road, I lay by the way-side in the bushes, waiting for him to come along. After a while he and his company came on sure enough,

c 2

1. This would be the fall of 1799.

2. This is an allusion to Jackson's "kitchen cabinet." Crockett refers to this group several times in the *Narrative,* and his letters more than once allude to Jackson as the superannuated old man surrounded by a group of creatures who ran the government for him. Jackson early in his term of office abandoned official cabinet meetings, and his policies were formed in meetings of the "kitchen cabinet." Among this group were W. B. Lewis, Amos Kendall, A. J. Donelson (Jackson's private secretary most of his term), John H. Eaton (secretary of war in the official cabinet until 1831), and Francis P. Blair (editor of the *Globe* who became a member after 1830).

and I pitched out from the bushes and set on him like a wild cat. I scratched his face all to a flitter jig, and soon made him cry out for quarters in good earnest. The fight being over, I went on home, and the next morning was started again to school; but do you think I went? No, indeed. I was very clear of it; for I expected the master would lick me up, as bad as I had the boy. So, instead of going to the schoolhouse, I laid out in the woods all day until in the evening the scholars were dismissed, and my brothers, who were also going to school, came along, returning home. I wanted to conceal this whole business from my father, and I therefore persuaded them not to tell on me, which they agreed to.

Things went on in this way for several days; I starting with them to school in the morning, and returning with them in the evening, but lying out in the woods all day. At last, however, the master wrote a note to my father, inquiring why I was not sent to school. When he read this note, he called me up, and I knew very well that I was in a devil of a hobble, for my father had been taking a few *horns,* and was in a good condition to make the fur fly. He called on me to know why I had not been at school? I told him I was afraid to go, and that the master would whip me ; for I knew quite well if I was turned over to this old Kitchen, I should be cooked up to a cracklin, in little or no time. But I soon found that I was not to expect a much better fate at home ; for my father told me, in a very angry manner, that he would whip me an eternal sight worse than the master, if I didn't start immediately to the school. I tried again to beg off ; but nothing would do, but to go to the school. Finding me rather too slow about starting, he gathered about a two year old hickory, and broke after me. I put out with all my might, and soon we were both up to the top of our speed. We had a tolerable tough race for about a mile ; but mind me, not on the school-house road, for I was trying to get as far the t'other way as possible. And I yet believe, if my father and the schoolmaster could both have levied on me about that time, I should never have been called on to sit in the councils of the nation, for I think they would have used me up. But fortunately for me, about this time, I saw just before me a hill, over which I made headway, like a young steamboat. As soon as I had passed over it, I turned to one side, and hid myself in the bushes. Here I waited until the old gentleman passed by, puffing and blowing, as tho' his steam

3. Steamboat and river terminology, later to be employed by Mark Twain.

4. "Cut out," one of the characteristic expressions in the *Narrative*, occurs 24 times, and counting variations (e.g., "put out") the number goes well over 30. It does not occur, however, in Crockett's letters. It was used in a letter written in 1827 by Crockett's son, John W., from Paris, Tenn., when John was only 19 years old, and therefore may have been good local idiom in West Tennessee at that time. Chilton was also from the West, so he may have added the expression to the book.

5. Crockett's short course in education smacks so much of Daniel Boone's course that one is a bit skeptical about Crockett's. In Boone's case, he fought the schoolteacher himself, and so could not "get an education."

6. It is unknown which of his four elder brothers is meant here. Torrence, *Crockett*, 4, gives the name of the eldest brother as John, born about 1777, followed by James, William, and Wilson, about 1779, 1782, and 1784, and a younger brother, Joseph, about 1788; the three sisters, Betsy, Jane, and Sally, were born about 1790, 1792, and 1794, respectively. *Cf.* French and Armstrong, *Crockett Family*, 329, who omit the name of the eldest, but say he was born in 1778 or 1779; followed by James, born 1780; William, born 1782; and Wilson, born 1784.

7. Wythe County.

8. Chilton must have failed to cross his *t* here; succeeding editions employ *tie*. The reference is to the early custom of "leap frog" riding: when two men traveled with one horse, one would ride a certain distance, tie the mount, and walk on; then the other rider would repeat the same action.

was high enough to burst his boilers.[8] I waited until he gave up the hunt, and passed back again : I then cut out,[4] and went to the house of an acquaintance a few miles off, who was just about to start with a drove. His name was Jesse Cheek, and I hired myself to go with him, determining not to return home, as home and the school-house[5] had both become too hot for me. I had an elder brother,[6] who also hired to go with the same drove. We set out and went on through Abbingdon, and the county seat of Withe[7] county, in the state of Virginia ; and then through Lynchburgh, by Orange court-house, and Charlottesville, passing through what was called Chester Gap, on to a town called Front Royal, where my employer sold out his drove to a man by the name of Vanmetre ; and I was started homeward again, in company with a brother of the first owner of the drove, with one horse between us ; having left my brother to come on with the balance of the company.

I traveled on with my new comrade about three days' journey ; but much to his discredit, as I then thought, and still think, he took care all the time to ride, but never to lie ;[8] at last I told him to go ahead, and I would come when I got ready. He gave me four dollars to bear my expenses upwards of four hundred miles, and then cut out and left me.

I purchased some provisions, and went on slowly, until at length I fell in with a waggoner, with whom I was disposed to scrape up a hasty acquaintance. I inquired where he lived, and where he was going, and all about his affairs. He informed me that he lived in Greenville, Tennessee, and was on his way to a place called Gerardstown, fifteen miles below Winchester. He also said, that after he should make his journey to that place, he would immediately return to Tennessee. His name was Adam Myers, and a jolly good fellow he seemed to be. On a little reflection, I determined to turn back and go with him, which I did; and we journeyed on slowly as waggons commonly do, but merrily enough. I often thought of home, and, indeed, wished bad enough to be there; but, when I thought of the school-house, and Kitchen, my master, and the race with my father, and the big hickory he carried, and of the fierceness of the storm of wrath that I had left him in, I was afraid to venture back; for I knew my father's nature so well, that I was certain his anger would hang on to him like a turkle[9] does to a fisherman's toe, and that, if I went back in a hurry, he would give me the devil in three or four ways.

9. Turtle.

10. Back in Crockett's era, monetary values were quite different from today's: land sold in East Tennessee for only 50 shillings per 100 acres; in West Tennessee, the poor land for as little as 12½ cents an acre. According to the Lincoln County Court Minutes, 1810 (copied by WPA), 13, the authorized prices for tavern keepers to charge were: "Good whiskey pr. half pint—12½ cents; Peach Brandy—12½ cents; West Indian Rum—25 cents; Dinner, breakfast, or supper—25 cents; Lodging—6½ cents; Stabledge, hay, or fodder for horse for 12 hours—25 cents; Corn per gallon—6½ cents."

But I and the waggoner had traveled two days, when we met my brother, who, I before stated, I had left behind when the drove was sold out. He persuaded me to go home, but I refused. He pressed me hard, and brought up a great many mighty strong arguments to induce me to turn back again. He pictured the pleasure of meeting my mother, and my sisters, who all loved me dearly, and told me what uneasiness they had already suffered about me. I could not help shedding tears, which I did not often do, and my affections all pointed back to those dearest friends, and as I thought, nearly the only ones I had in the world; but then the promised whipping—that was the thing. It came right slap down on every thought of home; and I finally determined that make or break, hit or miss, I would just hang on to my journey, and go ahead with the waggoner. My brother was much grieved at our parting, but he went his way, and so did I. We went on until at last we got to Gerardstown, where the waggoner tried to get a back load, but he could not without going to Alexandria. He engaged to go there, and I concluded that I would wait until he returned. I set in to work for a man by the name of John Gray, at twenty-five cents per day.[10] My labour, however, was light, such as ploughing in some small grain, in which I succeeded in pleasing the old man very well.   I continued working for him until the waggoner got back, and for a good long time afterwards, as he continued to run his team back and forward, hauling to and from Baltimore.   In the next spring,[11] from the proceeds of my daily labour, small as it was, I was able to get me some decent clothes, and concluded I would make a trip with the waggoner to Baltimore, and see what sort of a place that was, and what sort of folks lived there.   I gave him the balance of what money I had for safe keeping, which, as well as I recollect, was about seven dollars.   We got on well enough until we came near Ellicott's Mills.[12]   Our load consisted of flour, in barrels.   Here I got into the waggon for the purpose of changing my clothing, not thinking that I was in any danger ; but while I was in there we were met by some wheel-barrow men, who were working on the road, and the horses took a scare and away they went, like they had seen a ghost. They made a sudden wheel around, and broke the waggon tongue slap, short off, as a pipe-stem ; and snap went both of the axletrees at the same time, and of all devlish flouncing about of flour barrels that ever was seen, I reckon this took the beat. Even *a rat* would have stood a bad chance in a

11. If Crockett's account of time is accurate, this would be the spring of 1800.

12. Ellicott City.

straight race among them, and not much better in a crooked one ; for he would have been in a good way to be ground up as fine as ginger by their rolling over him. But this proved to me, that if a fellow is born to be hung, he will never be drowned ; and, further, that if he is born for a seat in Congress, even flour barrels can't make a mash of him. All these dangers I escaped unhurt, though, like most of the office-holders of these times,[13] for a while I was afraid to say my soul was my own ; for I didn't know how soon I should be knocked into a cocked hat, and get my walking papers for another country.

We put our load into another waggon, and hauled ours to a workman's shop in Baltimore, having delivered the flour, and there we intended to remain two or three days, which time was necessary to repair the runaway waggon. While I was there, I went, one day, down to the wharf, and was much delighted to see the big ships, and their sails all flying; for I had never seen any such things before, and, indeed, I didn't believe there were any such things in all nature. After a short time my curiosity induced me to step aboard of one, where I was met by the captain, who asked me if I didn't wish to take a voyage to London ? I told him I did, for by this time I had become pretty well weaned from home, and I cared but little where I was, or where I went, or what become of me. He said he wanted just such a boy as I was, which I was glad to hear. I told him I would go and get my clothes, and go with him. He enquired about my parents, where they lived, and all about them. I let him know that they lived in Tennessee, many hundred miles off. We soon agreed about my intended voyage, and I went back to my friend, the waggoner, and informed him that I was going to London,[14] and wanted my money and my clothes. He refused to let me have either, and swore that he would confine me, and take me back to Tennessee. I took it to heart very much, but he kept so close and constant a watch over me, that I found it impossible to escape from him, until he had started homeward, and made several days' journey on the road. He was, during this time, very ill to me, and threatened me with his waggon whip on several occasions. At length I resolved to leave him at all hazards; and so, before day, one morning, I got my clothes out of his waggon, and cut out, on foot, without a farthing of money to bear my expenses.[15] For all other friends having failed, I determined then to throw myself on Providence, and see how that would use me. I had gone, however, only a few

D

14. *Life and Adventures* covers in one chapter most of the first two chapters here. Discrepancies are minor: for instance, that book says that Crockett was asked to take a voyage to Liverpool, not London; that the companion gave him $3.00 to travel 400 miles rather than the $4.00 here; and that Crockett's failure to get an education was due to the fact that his father thought it impracticable. Incidentally, Crockett in the *Narrative* is much kinder toward his father than he was in *Life and Adventures*.

15. A farthing is an English coin worth one-fourth of a penny, or perhaps half a penny in the U.S. Money values varied with the section of the country, and a shilling might not bring in Tennessee what it brought in Virginia (about 17 cents, Crockett tells us later). English and American money terms are employed simultaneously at this period.

miles when I came up with another waggoner, and
such was my situation, that I felt more than ever
the necessity of endeavouring to find a friend. I
therefore concluded I would seek for one in him.
He was going westwardly, and very kindly enquired of me where I was travelling? My youth-
ful resolution, which had brooked almost every
thing else, rather gave way at this enquiry; for it
brought the loneliness of my situation, and every
thing else that was calculated to oppress me, directly to view. My first answer to his question
was in a sprinkle of tears, for if the world had
been given to me, I could not, at that moment,
have helped crying. As soon as the storm of
feeling was over, I told him how I had been treated
by the waggoner but a little before, who kept what
little money I had, and left me without a copper
to buy even a morsel of food.

He became exceedingly angry, and swore that
he would make the other waggoner give up my
money, pronouncing him a scoundrel, and many
other hard names. I told him I was afraid to see
him, for he had threatened me with his waggon
whip, and I believed he would injure me. But
my new friend was a very large, stout-looking
man, and as resolute as a tiger. He bid me
not to be afraid, still swearing he would have

my money, or whip it out of the wretch who had it.

We turned and went back about two miles, when we reached the place where he was. I went reluctantly; but I depended on my friend for protection. When we got there, I had but little to say; but approaching the waggoner, my friend said to him, "You damn'd rascal, you have treated this boy badly." To which he replied, it was my fault. He was then asked, if he did not get seven dollars of my money, which he confessed. It was then demanded of him; but he declared most solemnly, that he had not that amount in the world; that he had spent my money, and intended paying it back to me when we got to Tennessee. I then felt reconciled, and persuaded my friend to let him alone, and we returned to his waggon, geared up, and started. His name I shall never forget while my memory lasts; it was Henry Myers.[16] He lived in Pennsylvania, and I found him what he professed to be, a faithful friend and a clever fellow.

We traveled together for several days, but at length I concluded to endeavour to make my way homeward; and for that purpose set out again on foot, and alone. But one thing I must not omit. The last night I staid with Mr. Myers, was at a

16. A coincidence that both of these waggoners should be named Myers—one Adam, the other Henry.

place where several other waggoners also staid. He told them, before we parted, that I was a poor little straggling boy, and how I had been treated ; and that I was without money, though I had a long journey before me, through a land of stran gers, where it was not even a wilderness.

They were good enough to contribute a sort of money-purse, and presented me with three dol lars. On this amount I travelled as far as Mont gomery court-house, in the state of Virginia, where it gave out. I set in to work for a man by the name of James Caldwell, a month, for five dollars, which was about a shilling a day. When this time was out, I bound myself to a man by the name of Elijah Griffith, by trade a hatter, agree ing to work for him four years. I remained with him about eighteen months, when he found him self so involved in debt, that he broke up, and left the country.[17] For this time I had received nothing, and was, of course, left without money, and with but very few clothes, and them very indifferent ones. I, however, set in again, and worked about as I could catch employment, until I got a little money, and some clothing ; and once more cut out for home. When I reached New River, at the mouth of a small stream, called Little River, the white caps were flying so, that I couldn't

17. Following the chronology, this must be in early 1802.

not get any body to attempt to put me across. I argued the case as well as I could, but they told me there was great danger of being capsized, and drowned, if I attempted to cross. I told them if I could get a canoe I would venture, caps or no caps. They tried to persuade me out of it; but finding they could not, they agreed I might take a canoe, and so I did, and put off. I tied my clothes to the rope of the canoe, to have them safe, whatever might happen. But I found it a mighty ticklish business, I tell you. When I got out fairly on the river, I would have given the world, if it had belonged to me, to have been back on shore. But there was no time to lose now, so I just determined to do the best I could, and the devil take the hindmost. I turned the canoe across the waves, to do which, I had to turn it nearly up the river, as the wind came from that way; and I went about two miles before I could land. When I struck land, my canoe was about half full of water, and I was as wet as a drowned rat. But I was so much rejoiced, that I scarcely felt the cold, though my clothes were frozen on me; and in this situation, I had to go above three miles, before I could find any house, or fire to warm at. I, however, made out to get to one at last, and then I thought I would warm the inside

18. Sullivan County was formed in 1779 largely from territory previously thought to belong to Virginia. Crockett's father John owned land there by North Carolina Land Grant No. 179, Oct. 10, 1783, Sullivan County Deed Books (copied by WPA), I, 544. He probably lived there before moving to Greene prior to 1786 (the year of David's birth), but did not sell the home place until June 4, 1787, the deed of warranty being signed by both John and Rebeckah Crockett. *Ibid.*, 218. David's brother, with whom he stayed, probably was visiting their father's younger brother, Joseph, who owned land in Sullivan. *Ibid.*, II and III, *passim*.

19. If our count of time is correct, Crockett left in the fall of 1799 and returned in early spring 1802 —a long time indeed for a young man almost 16.

20. According to Torrence, *Crockett*, 4, her name was Betsy.

a little, as well as the outside, that there might be no grumbling.

So I took "a leetle of the creater,"—that warmer of the cold, and cooler of the hot,—and it made me feel so good that I concluded it was like the negro's rabbit, " good any way." I passed on until I arrived in Sullivan county, in the state of Tennessee, and there I met with my brother, who had gone with me when I started from home with the cattle drove. [18]

I staid with him a few weeks, and then went on to my father's, which place I reached late in the evening. Several waggons were there for the night, and considerable company about the house. I enquired if I could stay all night, for I did not intend to make myself known, until I saw whether any of the family would find me out. I was told that I could stay, and went in, but had mighty little to say to any body. I had been gone so long, and had grown so much, that the family did not at first know me.[19] And another, and perhaps a stronger reason was, they had no thought or expectation of me, for they all long given me up for finally lost.

After a while, we were all called to supper. I went with the rest. We had sat down to the table and begun to eat, when my eldest sister recollected [20] me : she sprung up, ran and seized me around the neck, and exclaimed, " Here is my lost brother."

My feelings at this time it would be vain and foolish for me to attempt to describe. I had often thought I felt before, and I suppose I had, but sure I am, I never had felt as I then did. The joy of my sisters and my mother, and, indeed, of all the family, was such that it humbled me, and made me sorry that I hadn't submitted to a hundred whippings, sooner than cause so much affliction as they had suffered on my account.[21] I found the family had never heard a word of me from the time my brother left me. I was now almost *fifteen* years old;[22] and my increased age and size, together with the joy of my father, occasioned by my unexpected return, I was sure would secure me against my long dreaded whipping; and so they did. But it will be a source of astonishment to many, who reflect that I am now a member of the American Congress,—the most enlightened body of men in the world,—that at so advanced an age, the age of fifteen, I did not know the first letter in the book.[23]

21. One of the main differences between *Life and Adventures* and this *Narrative* is the family feeling Crockett puts in the latter.

22. There is a chronological error somewhere in the story, and it recurs later. The story so far has checked within a year, for Crockett would have been almost 16 if the "next fall" was 1799 and was followed by a spring, a summer, and 18 months with Elijah Griffith.

23. In the backwoods there was little time for "book-larnin'." Characteristic of the politics there was a lampooning of anything that suggested aristocratic tendencies. If a man could hunt, shoot, labor, and have a ready wit and good sportsmanship, he might well be proud of not having non-utilitarian accomplishments. Crockett was one of the earliest to help form a political pattern which lingers even today —many a politician has received votes by boasting that he is the man who is ignorant.

(45)

CHAPTER III.

I HAD remained for some short time[1] at home with my father, when he informed me that he owed a man, whose name was Abraham Wilson, the sum of thirty-six dollars, and that if I would set in and work out the note, so as to lift it for him, he would discharge me from his service, and I might go free. I agreed to do this, and went immediately to the man who held my father's note, and contracted with him to work six months for it. I set in, and worked with all my might, not losing a single day in the six months. When my time was out, I got my father's note, and then declined working with the man any longer, though he wanted to hire me mighty bad. The reason was, it was a place where a heap of bad company met to drink and gamble, and I wanted to get away from them, for I know'd[2] very well if I staid there, I should get a bad name, as nobody could be respectable that would live there. I therefore returned to my father, and gave him up his paper,

1. The year must have been 1802, though according to Crockett he was only 15 years old.

2. Chilton uses this type of grammatical error to exemplify the inaccuracies of Crockett's speech, yet this type is rare in Crockett's letters. Crockett's errors usually are varying subject and verb number and using an adjective for an adverb. His use of the past participle for the past tense (in corrupted form—as here, "I know'd") is so infrequent as to be negligible. Occasionally in the letters the past tense is used for the past participle ("you have saw," and "I have wrote"), but this and disagreement of subject and verb rarely occur in the *Narrative*.

3. Records of John Crockett's debts are numerous. In addition to the enforced sale of his land, other debts of varying amounts were recorded. One, in an inventory of the personal estate of Gideon Morriss, was "John Crockett's Note for 35 Bushels Indian corn-17 Sept. 1783-Desperate." Jefferson County Will Book, No. 1, 1792–1810 (copied by WPA), 176 (May 9, 1798).

4. No information directly relevant to this person has been found. There is, however, a record of an earlier debt to a Daniel Kennedy, clerk of the court, state of Franklin, dated May 26, 1787: "Sir: Be pleased to Pay the Bearer Daniel Kennedy One Pound Franklin money and you will Oblige——yours &c John Crockett. Capt. John Tadlock." A photographic reproduction of this document is given in Reynolds, "Crockett Family," 188.

5. *Life and Adventures* states that the amount was $30.

which seemed to please him mightily, for though he was poor,[3] he was an honest man, and always tried mighty hard to pay off his debts.

I next went to the house of an honest old Quaker, by the name of John Kennedy,[4] who had removed from North Carolina, and proposed to hire myself to him, at two shillings a day. He agreed to take me a week on trial; at the end of which he appeared pleased with my work, and informed me that he held a note on my father for forty dollars,[5] and that he would give me that note if I would work for him six months. I was certain enough that I should never get any part of the note; but then I remembered it was my father that owed it, and I concluded it was my duty as a child to help him along, and ease his lot as much as I could. I told the Quaker I would take him up at his offer, and immediately went to work. I never visited my father's house during the whole time of this engagement, though he lived only fifteen miles off. But when it was finished, and I had got the note, I borrowed one of my employer's horses, and, on a Sunday evening, went to pay my parents a visit. Some time after I got there, I pulled out the note and handed it to my father, who supposed Mr. Kennedy had sent it for collection. The old man looked mighty sorry, and said to me he had not the money to pay it, and didn't know what he should do. I then told him I had paid it for him, and it was then his own; that it was not presented for collection, but as a present from me. At this, he shed a heap of tears; and as soon as he got a little over it, he said he was sorry he couldn't give me any thing, but he was not able, he was too poor.

The next day, I went back to my old friend, the Quaker, and set in to work for him for some clothes; for I had now worked a year[6] without getting any money at all, and my clothes were nearly all worn out, and what few I had left were mighty indifferent. I worked in this way for about two months; and in that time a young woman from North Carolina, who was the Quaker's niece, came on a visit to his house. And now I am just getting on a part of my history that I know I never can forget. For though I have heard people talk about hard loving, yet I reckon no poor devil in this world was ever cursed with such hard love as mine has always been, when it came on me. I soon found myself head over heels in love with this girl, whose name the public could make no use of; and I thought that if all the hills about there were pure chink,[7] and all be-

6. This would be "a short time at home" plus one year of work—from spring 1802, to about summer 1803.

7. From the sound of metal coins, which were preferred to paper money in a time of inflated currency. "Pure chink" would mean, then, pure silver or gold—and more likely the latter.

8. This is the first of many aphorisms (e.g., "choak me like a cold potatoe"; "cake was dough"; "safety pipes enough"; "nigh to burst my boilers") on about the next 10 pages. Because the aphorisms then cease abruptly, it would seem that the authors soon tired of their word-game.

9. A similar phrase was attributed by Seba Smith to "Major Jack Downing" in his preface to *Life of Downing*, v. Possibly the repetition in the *Narrative* indicates nothing more than mimicking that very popular work.

longed to me, I would give them if I could just talk to her as I wanted to; but I was afraid to begin, for when I would think of saying any thing to her, my heart would begin to flutter like a duck in a puddle;[8] and if I tried to outdo it and speak, it would get right smack up in my throat, and choak me like a cold potatoe. It bore on my mind in this way, till at last I concluded I must die if I didn't broach the subject; and so I determined to begin and hang on a trying to speak, till my heart would get out of my throat one way or t'other. And so one day at it I went, and after several trials I could say a little. I told her how well I loved her; that she was the darling object of my soul and body; and I must have her, or else I should pine down to nothing, and just die away with the consumption.

I found my talk was not disagreeable to her; but she was an honest girl, and didn't want to deceive nobody. She told me she was engaged to her cousin, a son of the old Quaker. This news was worse to me than war, pestilence, or famine; but still I knowed I could not help myself. I saw quick enough my cake was dough,[9] and I tried to cool off as fast as possible; but I had hardly safety pipes enough, as my love was so hot as mighty nigh to burst my boilers. But I didn't press my claims any more, seeing there was no chance to do any thing.

I began now to think, that all my misfortunes growed out of my want of learning. I had never been to school but four days, as the reader has already seen, and did not yet know a letter.

I thought I would try to go to school some ; and as the Quaker had a married son,[10] who was living about a mile and a half from him, and keeping a school, I proposed to him that I would go to school four days in the week, and work for him the other two, to pay my board and schooling. He agreed I might come on those terms ; and so at it I went, learning and working back and forwards, until I had been with him nigh on to six months.[11] In this time I learned to read a little in my primer, to write my own name,[12] and to cypher some in the three first rules in figures. And this was all the schooling I ever had in my life, up to this day. I should have continued longer, if it hadn't been that I concluded I couldn't do any longer without a wife ; and so I cut out to hunt me one.

I found a family of very pretty little girls that I had known when very young. They had lived in the same neighborhood with me, and I had thought very well of them. I made an offer to

E

10. In *Life and Adventures* the Quaker's son was the one visited by a female relative from North Carolina who had refused Crockett because of an offer from a "wealthy neighbor." Here it is not clear whether this married son is the one who married the girl Crockett "fell for" or not.

11. In *Life and Adventures* it was two days of work and three of school. Added to the summer of 1803, six months would mean about the first of 1804.

12. This is another example of his politically motivated exaggeration of his ignorance. Documentary proof that he could write his name two and one-half years later is his signature on his marriage bond. His correspondence attests that later he increased his writing ability.

13. Her name was Margaret Elder. Crockett is remarkably reticent about giving names, for he fails to name either of his wives or any of his children. Descendants of the Elders still live in Dandridge, Jefferson County.

14. Evidently, time passed during the courtship and if added to the previous accounting, it should be late 1804. On the other hand, the marriage license that was issued to Crockett is dated Oct. 21, 1805, when he was 19. The license, in the Jefferson County Marriage and Bond Book for 1792–1840, p. 53, Item No. 526, and now hanging on a wall of the Jefferson County courthouse in Dandridge, reads: "State of Tennessee—Jefferson County: To any licensed minister of the gospel or justice of the peace—Greeting: I do authorize and empower you to celebrate the rite of marriage between David Crockett and Margaret Elder and join them together as husband and wife. Given at my office in Dandridge, the 21st day of October, 1805. J. Hamilton, Clerk." The marriage, however, never took place, as Crockett later tells us.

15. This rifle, later used in partial payment to a Quaker for a horse, is now owned by a descendant of the Quaker, Samuel Gwin, of Modesto, Calif. Another gun, given to Crockett by Whigs in Philadelphia on his Boston tour in 1834 (and so engraved), is now in possession of Mrs. A. Sidney (Beth) Holderness, Crockett's great-great-granddaughter. Shackford, *Crockett*, 309. Contrary to some accounts, Crockett did not take this gun to Texas as was alleged in ch. III of *Texas Exploits*. Although *Life and Adventures* re-

one of them, whose name is nobody's business,[13] no more than the Quaker girl's was, and I found she took it very well. I still continued paying my respects to her, until I got to love her as bad as I had the Quaker's niece ; and I would have agreed to fight a whole regiment of wild cats if she would only have said she would have me. Several months passed in this way, during all of which time she continued very kind and friendly. At last, the son of the old Quaker and my first girl had concluded to bring their matter to a close, and my little queen and myself were called on to wait on them. We went on the day, and performed our duty as attendants. This made me worse than ever ; and after it was over, I pressed my claim very hard on her, but she would still give me a sort of an evasive answer. However, I gave her mighty little peace, till she told me at last she would have me. I thought this was glorification enough, even without spectacles. I was then about eighteen years old.[14] We fixed the time to be married ; and I thought if that day come, I should be the happiest man in the created world, or in the moon, or any where else.

I had by this time got to be mighty fond of the rifle, and had bought a capital one.[15] I most generally carried her with me whereever I went, and though I had got back to the old Quaker's to live, who was a very particular man, I would sometimes slip out and attend the shooting matches, where they shot for beef; I always tried, though, to keep it a secret from him. He had at the same time a bound boy living with him, who I had gotten into almost as great a notion of the girls as myself. He was about my own age, and was deeply smitten with the sister to my intended wife. I know'd it was in vain to try to get the leave of the old man for my young associate to go with me on any of my courting frolics; but I thought I could fix a plan to have him along, which would not injure the Quaker, as we had no notion that he should ever know it. We commonly slept up-stairs, and at the gable end of the house there was a window. So one Sunday, when the old man and his family were all gone to meeting, we went out and cut a long pole, and, taking it to the house, we set it up on end in the corner, reaching up the chimney as high as the window. After this we would go up-stairs to bed, and then putting on our Sunday clothes, would go out at the window, and climb down the pole, take a horse apiece, and ride about ten miles to where his sweetheart lived, and the girl I claimed as my wife. I was always mighty

fers to a Crockett rifle as "beautiful Betsy," the *Narrative* never uses the name. The "Crockett" gun on display in the Alamo is engraved: "Presented to David Crockett at Nashville, Tenn. 1822." According to W. H. Barnett in a letter to the Hon. Jno. W. Crockett (David's great-grandson), Feb. 5, 1910, the gun was sold soon after the Alamo massacre by John W. Crockett (David's eldest son) to a close friend of David's, Wade H. Hall of Alabama, and acquired by Barnett (whose father had been a close friend of both Hall and Crockett) in 1860 from Hall's son. Although the "Hon. Jno. W." owned the gun for a time, he wrote in 1914: "I have never been satisfied fully that my great grandfather ever owned it, . . . although he may have." Both letters are quoted in Cooper, "Some Crockett Firearms," 62–69, which also has a picture of the gun.

16. This expression is employed seven times in the *Narrative*. It or a similar one appears also in Crockett's letters, but not precisely in the same sense because he omits "there are." One letter (from Texas, to Margaret and Wiley Flowers, Jan. 9, 1836) has: "plenty of timber," "game aplenty," and "bees and honey plenty."

17. "Real grit"—in the real chink—gold or silver. Crockett was mistaken about banknotes; paper money had been in use even during the colonial period. There was no bank in Tennessee, however, until 1807 and not in East Tennessee until 1811. This sentence is one of the few in the *Narrative* having a plural noun with a singular verb.

18. Apparently the marriage was supposed to take place on Oct. 24, 1805, a Thursday. *Life and Adventures* attributes the unfulfillment of Crockett's marriage plans to his failure to show up on the proposed day because he attended a "frolic," and implies that Crockett was negligent, got drunk, and invited his jilting (ch. II, p. 33).

careful to be back before day, so as to escape being found out ; and in this way I continued my attentions very closely until a few days before I was to be married, or at least thought I was, for I had no fear that any thing was about to go wrong.

Just now I heard of a shooting-match in the neighbourhood, right between where I lived and my girl's house; and I determined to kill two birds with one stone,—to go to the shooting match first, and then to see her. I therefore made the Quaker believe I was going to hunt for deer, as they were pretty plenty[16] about in those parts ; but, instead of hunting them, I went straight on to the shooting-match, where I joined in with a partner, and we put in several shots for the beef. I was mighty lucky, and when the match was over I had won the whole beef. This was on a Saturday, and my success had put me in the finest humour in the world. So I sold my part of the beef for five dollars in the real grit, for I believe that was before bank-notes was invented ; at least, I had never heard of any.[17] I now started on to ask for my wife ; for, though the next Thursday was our wedding day, I had never said a word to her parents about it.[18] I had always dreaded the undertaking so bad, that I had put the evil hour off as long as possible ; and, indeed, I calculated they knowed me so well, they wouldn't raise any objection to having me for their son-in-law. I had a great deal better opinion of myself, I found, than other people had of me ; but I moved on with a light heart, and my five dollars jingling in my pocket, thinking all the time there was but few greater men in the world than myself.

In this flow of good humour I went ahead, till I got within about two miles of the place, when I concluded I would stop awhile at the house of the girl's uncle ; where I might enquire about the family, and so forth, and so on.[19] I was indeed just about ready to consider her uncle, my uncle ; and her affairs, my affairs. When I went in, tho', I found her sister there. I asked how all was at home ? In a minute I found from her countenance something was wrong. She looked mortified, and didn't answer as quick as I thought she ought, being it was her *brother-in-law* talking to her. However, I asked her again. She then burst into tears, and told me her sister was going to deceive me ; and that she was to be married to another man the next day. This was as sudden to me as a clap of thunder of a bright sunshiny day. It was the cap-stone of all the afflictions I had ever

E 2

19. Rourke, *Davy Crockett*, 25, through a misuse of sources, says that Crockett was told by some men at the girl's home that "the fickle young woman had ridden away to Kentucky with a man she had married the day before."

met with ; and it seemed to me, that it was more than any human creature could endure. It struck me perfectly speechless for some time, and made me feel so weak, that I thought I should sink down. I however recovered from my shock after a little, and rose and started without any ceremony, or even bidding any body good-bye. The young woman followed me out to the gate, and entreated me to go on to her father's, and said she would go with me. She said the young man, who was going to marry her sister, had got his license, and had asked for her ; but she assured me her father and mother both preferred me to him ; and that she had no doubt but that, if I would go on, I could break off the match. But I found I could go no further. My heart was bruised, and my spirits were broken down ; so I bid her farewell, and turned my lonesome and miserable steps back again homeward, concluding that I was only born for hardships, misery, and disappointment. I now began to think, that in making me, it was entirely forgotten to make my mate ; that I was born odd, and should always remain so, and that nobody would have me.

But all these reflections did not satisfy my mind, for I had no peace day nor night for several weeks. My appetite failed me, and I grew daily worse and worse. They all thought I was sick; and so I was. And it was the worst kind of sickness,—a sickness of the heart, and all the tender parts, produced by disappointed love.

CHAPTER IV.

I CONTINUED in this down-spirited situation for a good long time,[1] until one day I took my rifle and started a hunting. While out, I made a call at the house of a Dutch widow, who had a daughter that was well enough as to smartness, but she was as ugly as a stone fence. She was, however, quite talkative, and soon begun to laugh at me about my disappointment.

She seemed disposed, though, to comfort me as much as she could ; and, for that purpose, told me to keep in good heart, that " there was as good fish in the sea as had ever been caught out of it." I doubted this very much ; but whether or not, I was certain that she was not one of them, for she was so homely that it almost give me a pain in the eyes to look at her.

But I couldn't help thinking, that she had intended what she had said as a banter for me to court her ! ! !—the last thing in creation I could

1. "A good long time" meant less than nine months, for within this period he again wooed—and this time won.

have thought of doing. I felt little inclined to talk on the subject, it is true ; but, to pass off the time, I told her I thought I was born odd, and that no fellow to me could be found. She protested against this, and said if I would come to their reaping, which was not far off, she would show me one of the prettiest little girls there I had ever seen. She added that the one who had deceived me was nothing to be compared with her. I didn't believe a word of all this, for I had thought that such a piece of flesh and blood as she was had never been manufactured, and never would again. I agreed with her, though, that the little varment had treated me so bad, that I ought to forget her, and yet I couldn't do it. I concluded the best way to accomplish it was to cut out again, and see if I could find any other that would answer me ; and so I told the Dutch girl I would be at the reaping, and would bring as many as I could with me.

I employed my time pretty generally in giving information of it, as far as I could, until the day came ; and I then offered to work for my old friend, the Quaker, two days, if he would let his bound boy go with me one to the reaping. He refused, and reproved me pretty considerable roughly for my proposition ; and said, if he was in my place he wouldn't go ; that there would be a great deal of bad company there ; and that I had been so good a boy, he would be sorry for me to get a bad name. But I knowed my promise to the Dutch girl, and I was resolved to fulfil it ; so I shouldered my rifle, and started by myself. When I got to the place, I found a large company of men and women, and among them an old Irish woman,[2] who had a great deal to say. I soon found out from my Dutch girl, that this old lady was the mother of the little girl she had promised me, though I had not yet seen her. She was in an out-house with some other youngsters, and had not yet made her appearance. Her mamma, however, was no way bashful. She came up to me, and began to praise my red cheeks,[3] and said she had a sweetheart for me. I had no doubt she had been told what I come for, and all about it. In the evening I was introduced to her daughter, and I must confess, I was plaguy well pleased with her from the word go. She had a good countenance, and was very pretty, and I was full bent on making up an acquaintance with her.

It was not long before the dancing commenced, and I asked her to join me in a reel. She very readily consented to do so ; and after we had finished our dance, I took a seat alongside of

2. This statement is probably accurate. Her maiden name was Jean Kennedy. She had married William Finley, of Scotch-Irish descent, in 1786. Torrence, *Crockett*, 5–6. French and Armstrong, *Crockett Family*, 384, trace the Finleys' line of descent "back to the House of Macbeth."

3. In Crockett's letter to James Blackburn, Feb. 5, 1828 (THS), he mourns that, after being ill for some time and being bled by the doctor, who took two quarts of blood from him at one time, "I am much reduced in flesh and have lost all my Red Rosy Cheeks that I have carryed So many years."

4. Both the *Dictionary of American English* and
Stevenson's *Book of Proverbs* credit the expression
to the "Autobiography," but list the publication date
of the book as 1823.

her, and entered into a talk. I found her very
interesting ; while I was setting by her, making
as good a use of my time as I could, her mother
came to us, and very jocularly called me her son-
in-law. This rather confused me, but I looked on
it as a joke of the old lady, and tried to turn it off
as well as I could ; but I took care to pay as
much attention to her through the evening as I
could. I went on the old saying, of salting the
cow to catch the calf.[4] I soon become so much
pleased with this little girl, that I began to think
the Dutch girl had told me the truth, when she
said there was still good fish in the sea.

We continued our frolic till near day, when
we joined in some plays, calculated to amuse
youngsters. I had not often spent a more agreeable
night. In the morning, however, we all had to
part ; and I found my mind had become much better reconciled than it had been for a long time.
I went home to the Quaker's, and made a bargain
to work with his son for a low-priced horse. He
was the first one I had ever owned, and I was to
work six months for him. I had been engaged
very closely five or six weeks, when this little
girl run in my mind so, that I concluded I must
go and see her, and find out what sort of people
they were at home. I mounted my horse and

away I went to where she lived, and when I got there I found her father a very clever[5] old man, and the old woman as talkative as ever. She wanted badly to find out all about me, and as I thought to see how I would do for her girl. I had not yet seen her about, and I began to feel some anxiety to know where she was.

In a short time, however, my impatience was relieved, as she arrived at home from a meeting to which she had been.[6] There was a young man with her, who I soon found was disposed to set up claim to her, as he was so attentive to her that I could hardly get to slip in a word edgeways. I began to think I was barking up the wrong tree again; but I was determined to stand up to my rack, fodder or no fodder.[7] And so, to know her mind a little on the subject, I began to talk about starting, as I knowed she would then show some sign, from which I could understand which way the wind blowed.[8] It was then near night, and my distance was fifteen miles home. At this my little girl soon began to indicate to the other gentleman that his room[9] would be the better part of his company. At length she left him, and came to me, and insisted mighty hard that I should not go that evening; and, indeed, from all her actions and the attempts she made to get rid of him, I saw

F

5. *Clever* is still used in rural areas, at least in North Carolina, to mean *friendly or sociable*. Crockett's letter to George Patton, Oct. 31, 1835 (Mrs. Isabel Powell, Portland, Me.), uses the word in this sense.

6. *Life and Adventures* says Crockett fetched her from a neighbor's, where the story about the "stray bay filly" is told.

7. The letter to A. M. Hughes, Dec. 8, 1833, includes the phrase "to the Rack fodder." Variations of this phrase are used several times in the *Narrative*, but not in any letter prior to this date. Thus, this is perhaps an indication that Crockett was influenced by his perusal of the part of Chilton's manuscript that had been written prior to Dec. 8, 1833.

8. This error is not characteristic of Crockett's letters.

9. *Room* in this sense was in general use at that time. For example, for Nashville in the Cumberland Compact of 1780, a provision for the recall of local "judges" who should prove unsatisfactory to their constituents stated that their successors "shall have the same power with those in whose room . . . they are or may be chosen to act." Tennessee Historical Commission, *Three Pioneer Tennessee Documents* (Nashville, 1964), 13.

10. The earliest records on Crockett as a wolf hunter come later from West Tennessee. In those days, wolves were numerous and quite destructive of fowl and foal, and counties offered bounties for each mature wolf killed. There are many references to Crockett's being present as a member of the court when wolf scalps were brought in to be recorded and the killers rewarded in Lawrence County Court Minutes (copied by WPA), I (1818–23), 14–15. On the cover of this mutilated book (of which the first 11 pages are missing) is posted: "David Crockett J. P. Record 1818." Shackford, *Crockett*, 298.

11. That the elements would frighten a 20-year-old hunter is hardly credible. Very likely Chilton and Crockett repeated this bit of creative writing from *Life and Adventures* because it made a good story.

that she preferred me all holler.   But it wasn't long before I found trouble enough in another quarter.   Her mother was deeply enlisted for my rival, and I had to fight against her influence as well as his.   But the girl herself was the prize I was fighting for ; and as she welcomed me, I was determined to lay siege to her, let what would happen.   I commenced a close courtship, having cornered her from her old beau ; while he set off, looking on, like a poor man at a country frolic, and all the time almost gritting his teeth with pure disappointment.   But he didn't dare to attempt any thing more, for now I had gotten a start, and I looked at him every once in a while as fierce as a wild-cat.   I staid with her until Monday morning, and then I put out for home.

It was about two weeks after this that I was sent for to engage in a wolf hunt,[10] where a great number of men were to meet, with their dogs and guns, and where the best sort of sport was expected. I went as large as life, but I had to hunt in strange woods, and in a part of the country which was very thinly inhabited.   While I was out it clouded up, and I began to get scared ;[11] and in a little while I was so much so, that I didn't know which way home was, nor any thing about it.   I set out the way I thought it was, but it turned out with me,

as it always does with a lost man, I was wrong,
and took exactly the contrary direction from the
right one.   And for the information of young
hunters, I will just say, in this place, that whenever a fellow gets bad lost, the way home is just
the way he don't think it is.   This rule will hit
nine times out of ten.   I went ahead, though, about
six or seven miles, when I found night was coming
on fast ; but at this distressing time I saw a little
woman streaking it along through the woods like all
wrath, and so I cut on too, for I was determined
I wouldn't lose sight of her that night any more.
I run on till she saw me, and she stopped ; for she
was as glad to see me as I was to see her, as she
was lost as well as me.   When I came up to her,
who should she be but my little girl, that I had
been paying my respects to.   She had been out
hunting her father's horses, and had missed her
way, and had no knowledge where she was, or
how far it was to any house, or what way would
take us there.   She had been travelling all day,
and was mighty tired ; and I would have taken
her up, and toated her, if it hadn't been that I
wanted her just where I could see her all the
time, for I thought she looked sweeter than sugar ;
and by this time I loved her almost well enough
to eat her.

12. This gun transaction is extolled by the romancers.

13. The modern *infare*, a housewarming, especially one for a bride.

14. Here is a clear use of *clever* as "friendly" or "sociable."

At last I came to a path, that I know'd must go somewhere, and so we followed it, till we came to a house, at about dark. Here we staid all night. I set up all night courting ; and in the morning we parted. She went to her home, from which we were distant about seven miles, and I to mine, which was ten miles off.

I now turned in to work again ; and it was about four weeks before I went back to see her. I continued to go occasionally, until I had worked long enough to pay for my horse, by putting in my gun with my work,[12] to the man I had purchased from ; and then I began to count whether I was to be deceived again or not. At our next meeting we set the day for our wedding ; and I went to my father's, and made arrangements for an infair,[13] and returned to ask her parents for her. When I got there, the old lady appeared to be mighty wrathy ; and when I broached the subject, she looked at me as savage as a meat axe. The old man appeared quite willing, and treated me very clever.[14] But I hadn't been there long, before the old woman as good as ordered me out of her house. I thought I would put her in mind of old times, and see how that would go with her. I told her she had called me her son-in-law before I had attempted to call her my mother-in-law and I thought she ought to cool off. But her Irish was up too high to do any thing with her, and so I quit trying. All I cared for was, to have her daughter on my side, which I knowed was the case then; but how soon some other fellow might knock my nose out of joint again, I couldn't tell. I however felt rather insulted at the old lady, and I thought I wouldn't get married in her house. And so I told her girl, that I would come the next Thursday, and bring a horse, bridle, and saddle for her, and she must be ready to go. Her mother declared I shouldn't have her; but I know'd I should, if somebody else didn't get her before Thursday. I then started, bidding them good day, and went by the house of a justice of the peace,[15] who lived on the way to my father's, and made a bargain with him to marry me.

When Thursday came, all necessary arrangements were made at my father's to receive my wife; and so I took my eldest brother and his wife, and another brother, and a single sister that I had, and two other young men with me,[16] and cut out to her father's house to get her. We went on, until we got within two miles of the place, where we met a large company that had heard of the wedding, and were waiting.[17] Some of that company went on with my brother and sis-

15. A little later, he says he was married by a "parson."

16. Torrence, *Crockett*, 4, says that the eldest brother's name was John, but whom he married is unknown; his sisters were Betsy, Jane, and Sally; either James, William, or Wilson was "another brother." One of the two other young men was doubtless Thomas Doggett, inasmuch as he had served as Crockett's bondsman. Crockett's bond reads: "Know all men by those presents that we David Crockett and Thomas Doggett are held and firmly bound unto John Sevier Governor and his successors in office in the sum of Twelve hundred & fifty Dollars to be void on condition there be no cause to obstruct the marriage of the said David Crockett with Polly Findley [*sic*] witness our hands and seals the 12th day of August 1806 . . . ." As Aug. 12, 1806, was a Tuesday, the wedding was supposed to take place on Thur., Aug. 14, 1806.

17. According to legend, the custom in certain localities was to send "envoys" ahead as the wedding party approached the destination. If the envoys were well received—that is, if their empty flasks or flagons were filled—all was well, and the envoys returned on the run to the wedding group. The liquor was forthwith consumed by the party.

18. Alight or mount.

ter, and the young man I had picked out to wait on me. When they got there, they found the old lady as wrathy as ever. However the old man filled their bottle, and the young men returned in a hurry. I then went on with my company, and when I arrived I never pretended to dismount from my horse, but rode up to the door, and asked the girl if she was ready ; and she said she was. I then told her to light[18] on the horse I was leading ; and she did so. Her father, though, had gone out to the gate, and when I started he commenced persuading me to stay and marry there ; that he was entirely willing to the match, and that his wife, like most women, had entirely too much tongue ; but that I oughtn't to mind her. I told him if she would ask me to stay and marry at her house, I would do so. With that he sent for her, and after they had talked for some time out by themselves, she came to me and looked at me mighty good, and asked my pardon for what she had said, and invited me stay. She said it was the first child she had ever had to marry ; and she couldn't bear to see her go off in that way ; that if I would light, she would do the best she could for us. I couldn't stand every thing, and so I agreed, and we got down, and went in. I sent off then for my parson, and got married in a short time ;[19] for I was afraid to wait long, for fear of another defeat. We had as good treatment as could be expected ; and that night all went on well. The next day we cut out for my father's, where we met a large company of people, that had been waiting a day and a night for our arrival. We passed the time quite merrily, until the company broke up ; and having gotten my wife, I thought I was completely made up, and needed nothing more in the whole world. But I soon found this was all a mistake—for now having a wife, I wanted every thing else ; and, worse than all, I had nothing to give for it.

I remained a few days at my father's, and then went back to my new father-in-law's ; where, to my surprise, I found my old Irish mother in the finest humour in the world.

She gave us two likely cows and calves, which, though it was a small marriage-portion, was still better than I had expected, and, indeed, it was about all I ever got. I rented a small farm and cabin, and went to work ; but I had much trouble to find out a plan to get any thing to put in my house. At this time, my good old friend the Quaker came forward to my assistance, and gave me an order to a store for fifteen dollars' worth of such things as my little wife might choose. With

19. Since the marriage is recorded in Jefferson County as of Aug. 16, 1806, instead of Aug. 14, two days intervened between the Finley squabble and the actual ceremony. Folmsbee and Catron, "Early Career," 63n.

20. John Wesley (b. July 10, 1807) and William (b. 1809). A daughter, Margaret (Polly) was born later. John Wesley was later to succeed his father in Congress after an interim of one term. Torrence, *Crockett*, 7–8. The will of William Finley, dated Apr. 3, 1818, and recorded in the Jefferson County Will Book, No. 2 (June session, 1819), 238, in addition to bequeathing $2.00 each to his sons William and Samuel and daughters Jean Barnes and Susannah Parks, also gave "to my daughter Mary Crockets three children John William and Polly two dollars each . . . ." The remainder of the estate was to go to his wife, Jean, "and son Kanneday," who were made executrix and executor. Obviously, the family was poor.

21. The southern part of Middle Tennessee, generally. The earliest settlement in this section was in Maury County, to the northwest, in 1808. A. W. Putnam, *History of Middle Tennessee* (Nashville, 1859; rpt. Knoxville, 1971), 569–73.

this, we fixed up pretty grand, as we thought, and allowed to get on very well. My wife had a good wheel, and knowed exactly how to use it. She was also a good weaver, as most of the Irish are, whether men or women; and being very industrious with her wheel, she had, in little or no time, a fine web of cloth, ready to make up; and she was good at that too, and at almost any thing else that a woman could do.

We worked on for some years, renting ground, and paying high rent, until I found it wan't the thing it was cracked up to be; and that I couldn't make a fortune at it just at all. So I concluded to quit it, and cut out for some new country. In this time we had two sons,[20] and I found I was better at increasing my family than my fortune. It was therefore the more necessary that I should hunt some better place to get along; and as I knowed I would have to move at some time, I thought it was better to do it before my family got too large, that I might have less to carry.

The Duck and Elk river country[21] was just beginning to settle, and I determined to try that. I had now one old horse, and a couple of two year old colts. They were both broke to the halter, and my father-in-law proposed, that, if I went, he would go with me, and take one horse to help me move. So we all fixed up, and I packed my two colts with as many of my things as they could bear ; and away we went across the mountains.[22] We got on well enough, and arrived safely in Lincoln county, on the head of the Mulberry fork of Elk river.[23] I found this a very rich country, and so new, that game, of different sorts, was very plenty. It was here that I began to distinguish myself as a hunter, and to lay the foundation for all my future greatness ; but mighty little did I know of what sort it was going to be. Of deer and smaller game I killed abundance ; but the bear had been much hunted in those parts before, and were not so plenty as I could have wished. I lived here in the years 1809 and '10, to the best of my recollection,[24] and then I moved to Franklin county, and settled on Bean creek, where I remained till after the close of the last war.[25]

22. The migration took place, probably late in Sept. or early Oct. 1811, for the Jefferson County Court Minutes, Nov. 5 (1810–11), 191, for Sept. 11, 181 (copied by WPA), state that Crockett was on that day a juror in the case of *Whitesides* v. *Outlaw.*

23. Lincoln County was created Nov. 14, 1809, from Bedford County, which was formed in 1807 from Rutherford. Foster, *Counties,* 67–68. Therefore the date of issuance of Crockett's first land warrant in Lincoln clears up the matter of when he moved, and the location of the county confirms his account of where he first settled. The entry of land, taken from Entry Book C, Surveyors District II, Entry No. 3944 (Tennessee State Library and Archives), 414, reads: "No. 3944. Surveyed. David Crockett, ass'ee of Wm. Gilchrist etc., by virtue of Certificate No. 849 for 320 Acres enters 5 acres of land in Lincoln County and on the head waters of the East fork of Mulberry Creek a North Branch of Elk River. BEGINNING at a Beech Marked D.C. Standing about 60 or 70 yards north eastwardly from S'd Crocketts house running thence West in Oblong and South for quantity, 25th., April 1812, including Sd Crocketts house and improvement, DAVID CROCKETT." Crockett must have been there several months at least. The next entry, 3945 (same date), for 15 acres on "the head Waters of the East fork of Mulberry Creek," was withdrawn, and in 1814 he was reported as delinquent on tax payment on the original five acres. Lincoln County Court Minutes (Nov. 1814), 124, 126. Crockett's delinquency was caused by his poverty, his absence at war, and his family's non-residence. The site is now in Moore County, formed from Lincoln and Franklin counties in 1871. Foster, *Counties,* 75.

24. The years should be 1811 and 1812.

25. The Creek War, or War of 1812. Bean (or

Bean's) Creek is about 10 miles due south of Winchester, the Franklin County seat. Because he evidently once considered moving to Kentucky, he called this home "Kentuck"; it was here that his wife Polly died and was buried. Both the home and the grave are commemorated by highway markers. McBride, "Crockett Memorials," 92–93.

CHAPTER V.

I WAS living ten miles below Winchester when the Creek war commenced ; and as military men are making so much fuss in the world at this time, I must give an account of the part I took in the defence of the country. If it should make me president,[1] why I can't help it ; such things will sometimes happen ; and my pluck is, never " to seek, nor decline office."[2]

It is true, I had a little rather not ; but yet, if the government can't get on without taking another president from Tennessee, to finish the work of " retrenchment and reform,"[3] why, then, I reckon I must go in for it. But I must begin about the war, and leave the other matter for the people to begin on.

The Creek Indians had commenced their open hostilities by a most bloody butchery at Fort Mines.[4] There had been no war among us for so long, that but few, who were not too old to bear arms, knew any thing about the business. I,

1. In Crockett's several references to himself and the presidency, there appears to be a vein of seriousness beneath his humor. As a matter of fact, he had been asked by the Mississippi Convention in Dec. 1833 to allow the use of his name as that of a candidate for President. Although this was likely a political maneuver to allow the state to hold her votes in reserve, Crockett probably took the request seriously. In addition, he and his ghost writer were quite aware that military fame enhanced a politician's chances.

2. A popular slogan of the day.

3. Two basic planks in Jackson's platform were economy and housecleaning of "grafters," and this phrase was perhaps the most distinctive slogan of the campaign. The result, however, was a spoils system nonpareil. This, of course, created more Jackson enemies. Crockett himself frequently and loosely used Jacksonian slogans in anti-Jackson ridicule.

4. Fort Mims. Crockett's statements that the Indians started the war was the usual white man's version.

for one, had often thought about war, and had
often heard it described ; and I did verily believe in my own mind, that I couldn't fight in
that way at all ; but my after experience convinced me that this was all a notion.   For when I
heard of the mischief which was done at the fort,
I instantly felt like going, and I had none of the
dread of dying that I expected to feel.   In a few
days a general meeting of the militia was called
for the purpose of raising volunteers ; and when
the day arrived for that meeting, my wife, who
had heard me say I meant to go to the war, began to beg me not to turn out.   She said she was
a stranger in the parts where we lived, had no
connexions living near her, and that she and our
little children would be left in a lonesome and
unhappy situation if I went away.   It was mighty
hard to go against such arguments as these ; but
my countrymen had been murdered, and I knew
that the next thing would be, that the Indians
would be scalping the women and children all
about there, if we didn't put a stop to it.   I rea-
soned the case with her as well as I could, and
told her, that if every man would wait till his
wife got willing for him to go to war, there would
be no fighting done, until we would all be killed
in our own houses ; that I was as able to go as

any man in the world ; and that I believed it was a duty I owed to my country. Whether she was satisfied with this reasoning or not, she did not tell me ; but seeing I was bent on it, all she did was to cry a little, and turn about to her work. The truth is, my dander was up, and nothing but war could bring it right again.

I went to Winchester, where the muster was to be, and a great many people had collected, for there was as much fuss among the people about the war as there is now about moving the deposites. When the men were paraded, a lawyer by the name of Jones addressed us, and closed by turning out himself, and enquiring, at the same time, who among us felt like we could fight Indians ? This was the same Mr. Jones who afterwards served in Congress, from the state of Tennessee.[5] He informed us he wished to raise a company, and that then the men should meet and elect their own officers. I believe I was about the second or third man that step'd out ; but on marching up and down the regiment a few times, we found we had a large company. We volunteered for sixty days,[6] as it was supposed our services would not be longer wanted. A day or two after this we met and elected Mr. Jones our captain, and also elected our other officers.[7] We

G

5. Capt. Francis Jones was a Tennessee representative to the 15th, 16th, and 17th U.S. Congresses, 1817–21. *Biographical Directory of Congress, 1774–1949*, p. 1385.

6. This is an intentional error; he signed up for 90 days, as shown by his service record: "24 Dec 1813. Muster Roll, Co. of Tennessee Volunteer Mounted Riflemen commanded by Capt. Francis Jones. Newton Cannon, Col. of Regt. Mustered till 24 Dec. 1813 . . . . [No. 18 on list] David Crockett, rank, private, date of enlistment 24 Sept 1813 to 24 Dec. 1813." Creek Indian War Muster and Pay Roll Records, War Records Division, National Archives; photostatic copies in Tennessee State Library and Archives, Vol. 3, Records of the War of 1812, Photo 11-C-1 (3). Crockett's statement was written to justify describing later his fictional part in the troop mutiny against Jackson.

7. In those days, officers in the militia were indeed elected.

then received orders to start on the next Monday week ; before which time, I had fixed as well as I could to go, and my wife had equip'd me as well as she was able for the camp. The time arrived ; I took a parting farewell of my wife and my little boys, mounted my horse, and set sail, to join my company. Expecting to be gone only a short time, I took no more clothing with me than I supposed would be necessary, so that if I got into an Indian battle, I might not be pestered with any unnecessary plunder, to prevent my having a fair shake with them. We all met and went ahead, till we passed Huntsville, and camped at a large spring called Bealy's spring.[8] Here we staid for several days, in which time the troops began to collect from all quarters. At last we mustered about thirteen hundred strong, all mounted volunteers, and all determined to fight, judging from myself, for I felt wolfish all over. I verily believe the whole army was of the real grit. Our captain didn't want any other sort ; and to try them he several times told his men, that if any of them wanted to go back home, they might do so at any time, before they were regularly mustered into the service. But he had the honour to command all his men from first to last, as not one of them left him.

8. Beaty's Spring, located a few miles south of Huntsville, Ala. This error was corrected in later editions.

Gen'l. Jackson had not yet left Nashville with his old foot volunteers, that had gone with him to Natchez in 1812, the year before.[9] While we remained at the spring, a Major Gibson[10] came, and wanted some volunteers to go with him across the Tennessee river and into the Creek nation, to find out the movements of the Indians. He came to my captain, and asked for two of his best woodsmen, and such as were best with a rifle. The captain pointed me out to him, and said he would be security that I would go as far as the major would himself, or any other man. I willingly engaged to go with him, and asked him to let me choose my own mate to go with me, which he said I might do. I chose a young man by the name of George Russell, a son of old Major Russell,[11] of Tennessee. I called him up, but Major Gibson said he thought he hadn't beard enough to please him,—he wanted men, and not boys. I must confess I was a little nettled at this; for I know'd George Russell, and I know'd there was no mistake in him; and I didn't think that courage ought to be measured by the beard, for fear a goat would have the preference over a man. I told the major he was on the wrong scent; that Russell could go as far as he could, and I must have him along. He saw I was a little wrathy, and said I had the best chance of

9. The date should be Jan. 1813. In 1812 Congress authorized a volunteer corps of 50,000 men to serve one year within a period of two years after they were organized. Jackson raised 2,500 men, and in Nov. 1812 they were accepted. At the close of 1812, with Jackson in command, they were ordered down the Ohio and Mississippi for defense of the lower states against the British, and possibly for invasion of Spanish-held West Florida. In Feb. 1813 Jackson was suddenly ordered to dismiss his volunteers and deliver all public property in his possession to Maj. Gen. James Wilkinson, regular army commander of that district. Suspecting a scheme to force his volunteers into joining the regular army, Jackson refused to obey the orders and set out on foot for Tennessee with his men. It was his iron determination and his toughness of physique on this journey which earned him the name of "Hickory," and then "Old Hickory." So great was the evidence to support Jackson's position that the administration in Washington, D. C., finally "approbated his conduct" and paid his troops. When the call came for troops for the Creek War, Gov. Willie Blount issued an order to call out 2,000 militia to rendezvous at Fayetteville. Some of those called were the troops of the previous enlistment, as Crockett says. S. Putnam Waldo, *Memoirs of Andrew Jackson*, 5th ed. (Hartford, 1820), 1–69.

10. Photostatic Records of the War of 1812 show that a John H. Gibson was second major under Col. John Coffee on Sept. 24, 1813.

11. As Crockett tells us later, Russell was not at this time a major but a captain. He had held the title of major in the local militia and retained it by courtesy.

12. Major Gibson.

13. On the Tennessee River, due south of Huntsville, Ala.

14. Evidently the Cherokee Indian colonel, Dick Brown, mentioned in ch. VI, is the same person. There was actually a Cherokee by that name in this group (Waldo, *Memoirs*, 70–75).

knowing, and agreed that it should be as I wanted it. He told us to be ready early in the morning for a start; and so we were. We took our camp equipage, mounted our horses, and, thirteen in number, including the major,[12] we cut out. We went on, and crossed the Tennessee river at a place called Ditto's Landing;[13] and then traveled about seven miles further, and took up camp for the night. Here a man by the name of John Haynes overtook us. He had been an Indian trader in that part of the nation, and was well acquainted with it. He went with us as a pilot. The next morning, however, Major Gibson and myself concluded we should separate and take different directions to see what discoveries we could make; so he took seven of the men, and I five, making thirteen in all, including myself. He was to go by the house of a Cherokee Indian, named Dick Brown,[14] and I was to go by Dick's father's; and getting all the information we could, we were to meet that evening where the roads came together, fifteen miles the other side of Brown's. At old Mr. Brown's I got a half blood Cherokee to agree to go with me, whose name was Jack Thompson. He was not then ready to start, but was to fix that evening, and overtake us at the fork road where I was to meet Major Gibson. I know'd it wouldn't be safe to camp right at the road ; and so I told Jack, that when he got to the fork he must holler like an owl, and I would answer him in the same way ; for I know'd it would be night before he got there. I and my men then started, and went on to the place of meeting, but Major Gibson was not there. We waited till almost dark, but still he didn't come. We then left the Indian trace[15] a little distance, and turning into the head of a hollow, we struck up camp. It was about ten o'clock at night, when I heard my owl, and I answered him. Jack soon found us, and we determined to rest there during the night. We staid also next morning till after breakfast : but in vain, for the major didn't still come.

I told the men we had set out to hunt a fight, and I wouldn't go back in that way ; that we must go ahead, and see what the red men were at. We started, and went to a Cherokee town about twenty miles off ; and after a short stay there, we pushed on to the house of a man by the name of Radcliff. He was a white man, but had married a Creek woman, and lived just in the edge of the Creek nation. He had two sons, large likely fellows, and a great deal of potatoes and corn, and, indeed, almost every thing else to go on ; so we

G 2

15. Trail or path. Their explorations before they return to camp take them about 65 miles into northeast Alabama, Crockett tells us later.

fed our horses and got dinner with him, and seemed to be doing mighty well. But he was bad scared all the time. He told us there had been ten painted warriors at his house only an hour before, and if we were discovered there, they would kill us, and his family with us. I replied to him, that my business was to hunt for just such fellows as he had described, and I was determined not to gack until I had done it. Our dinner being over, we saddled up our horses, and made ready to start. But some of my small company I found were disposed to return. I told them, if we were to go back then, we should never hear the last of it; and I was determined to go ahead. I knowed some of them would go with me, and that the rest were afraid to go back by themselves; and so we pushed on to the camp of some of the friendly Creeks, which was distant about eight miles. The moon was about the full, and the night was clear; we therefore had the benefit of her light from night to morning,[16] and I knew if we were placed in such danger as to make a retreat necessary, we could travel by night as well as in the day time.

We had not gone very far, when we met two negroes, well mounted on Indian ponies, and each with a good rifle. They had been taken from

16. This must have been the night of Oct. 6 and the morning of Oct. 7. According to Augustus De Morgan, *The Book of Almanacs* (London, 1851), 59, the moon was full on Oct. 10, 1813.

their owners by the Indians, and were running away from them, and trying to get back to their masters again. They were brothers, both very large and likely, and could talk Indian as well as English. One of them I sent on to Ditto's Landing, the other I took back with me. It was after dark when we got to the camp, where we found about forty men, women, and children.

They had bows and arrows, and I turned in to shooting with their boys by a pine light. In this way we amused ourselves very well for a while; but at last the negro, who had been talking to the Indians, came to me and told me they were very much alarmed, for the "red skins,"[17] as they called the war party of the Creeks, would come and find us there; and, if so, we should all be killed. I directed him to tell them that I would watch, and if one would come that night, I would carry the skin of his head home to make me a mockasin. When he made this communication, the Indians laughed aloud. At about ten o'clock at night we all concluded to try to sleep a little; but that our horses might be ready for use, as the treasurer said of the drafts on the United States' bank, on certain "contingences,"[18] we tied them up with our saddles on them, and every thing to our hand, if in the night our quarters should get uncomfort-

17. *Life and Adventures* and later editions of the *Narrative* use "red sticks" here. The term arose, according to Halbert and Ball, *Creek War*, 134n, because the hostile Creeks carried war clubs which "were invariably painted red. 'Red Stick' was considered an honorable appellation . . . . 'Red Stick War' is the name by which the war of 1813 is still known [1895] among the Creeks of the Indian Territory."

18. See the letter by R. B. Taney, acting secretary of the treasury, to the Hon. Andrew Stevenson, house speaker, Dec. 3, 1833, in which he submitted his report to Congress on his reasons for the removal of the deposits from the Bank of the United States. *Register of Debates in Congress*, X, pt. 4, app., 59 ff.

19. This was on the upper reaches of the river near present-day Gadsden, Ala. Fort Strother was built here and the Tallusahatchee (or Talluschatchie) Town massacre, which Crockett will soon describe, took place nearby.

able. We lay down with our guns in our arms, and I had just gotten into a dose of sleep, when I heard the sharpest scream that ever escaped the throat of a human creature. It was more like a wrathy painter than any thing else. The negro understood it, and he sprang to me; for tho' I heard the noise well enough, yet I wasn't wide awake enough to get up. So the negro caught me, and said the red sticks was coming. I rose quicker then, and asked what was the matter? Our negro had gone and talked with the Indian who had just fetched the scream, as he come into camp, and learned from him, that the war party had been crossing the Coosa river all day at the Ten islands;[19] and were going on to meet Jackson, and this Indian had come as a runner. This news very much alarmed the friendly Indians in camp, and they were all off in a few minutes. I felt bound to make this intelligence known as soon as possible to the army we had left at the landing; and so we all mounted our horses, and put out in a long lope to make our way back to that place. We were about sixty-five miles off. We went on to the same Cherokee town we had visited on our way out, having first called at Radcliff's, who was off with his family; and at the the town we found large fires burning, but not a

single Indian was to be seen.   They were all gone.
These circumstances were calculated to lay our
dander a little, as it appeared we must be in great
danger ; though we could easily have licked any
force of not more than five to one.   But we expected the whole nation would be on us, and
against such fearful odds we were not so rampant
for a fight.

We therefore staid only a short time in the light
of the fires about the town, preferring the light of
the moon and the shade of the woods. We pushed
on till we got again to old Mr. Brown's, which
was still about thirty miles from where we had
left the main army.   When we got there, the
chickens were just at the first crowing for day.
We fed our horses, got a morsel to eat ourselves,
and again cut out.   About ten o'clock in the
morning we reached the camp, and I reported to
Col. Coffee the news.[20] He didn't seem to mind
my report a bit, and this raised my dander higher
than ever ; but I knowed I had to be on my best
behaviour, and so I kept it all to myself ; though
I was so mad that I was burning inside like a tar-
kiln, and I wonder that the smoke hadn't been
pouring out of me at all points.

Major Gibson hadn't yet returned, and we all
began to think he was killed ; and that night they

20. Col. John Coffee was in charge of about 500
troops stationed near Huntsville. Waldo, *Memoirs*,
65–66.

21. Maj. Gibson arrived on Oct. 8, 1813. This was one of several incidents causing Crockett's inveterate hatred of army "brass"; he later argued in Congress against the regular army (as opposed to volunteers) and against West Point because of its aristocratic tendencies. Shackford, *Crockett*, 22–23.

22. On Oct. 8 Coffee informed Jackson that "from information derived from Indian runners, the hostile Creeks were in great force, and intended, simultaneously, to attack the frontiers of Georgia and Tennessee." On Oct. 10, Jackson took up the line of march and "reached Huntsville the same evening, a distance of from thirty to forty miles." Col. Coffee by this time had reached the Tennessee River, and it was not until the next day that Jackson overtook him, whereupon Jackson "dispatched colonel Coffee, with his mounted corps [including Crockett], to explore the river *Big* [Black] *Warrior*, and *Etomb-igaby*, commonly called Tombigbee." Waldo, *Memoirs*, 67–68, 72.

put out a double guard. The next day the major got in, and brought a worse tale than I had, though he stated the same facts, so far as I went. This seemed to put our colonel all in a fidget; and it convinced me, clearly, of one of the hateful ways of the world. When I made my report, it wasn't believed, because I was no officer; I was no great man, but just a poor soldier. But when the same thing was reported by Major Gibson ! ! why, then, it was all as true as preaching, and the colonel believed it every word.[21]

He, therefore, ordered breastworks to be thrown up, near a quarter of a mile long, and sent an express to Fayetteville, where General Jackson and his troops was, requesting them to push on like the very mischief, for fear we should all be cooked up to a cracklin before they could get there. Old Hickory-face made a forced march on getting the news; and on the next day, he and his men got into camp,[22] with their feet all blistered from the effects of their swift journey. The volunteers, therefore, stood guard altogether, to let them rest.

CHAPTER VI.

ABOUT eight hundred of the volunteers, and of
that number I was one, were now sent back, crossing
the Tennessee river, and on through Huntsville,
so as to cross the river again at another place,
and to get on the Indians in another direction.
After we passed Huntsville, we struck on the
river at the Muscle Shoals, and at a place on them
called Melton's Bluff. This river is here about
two miles wide, and a rough bottom ; so much
so, indeed, in many places, as to be dangerous ;
and in fording it this time, we left several of the
horses belonging to our men, with their feet fast in
the crevices of the rocks. The men, whose horses
were thus left, went ahead on foot. We pushed
on till we got to what was called the Black Warrior's town,[1] which stood near the very spot where
Tuscaloosa now stands, which is the seat of government for the state of Alabama.

This Indian town was a large one ; but when
we arrived we found the Indians had all left it.

1. On the headwaters of Black Warrior River.

2. *Leaves* is obviously an error of an unimaginative typesetter. Chilton's *b* must have looked like an *l* and his *n* a *v*. Succeeding editions have the correct *beans*.

3. The account of starvation rations is quite literal and, along with disputes over terms of enlistment, was a big factor in the mutinous conduct of the troops later on.

There was a large field of corn standing out, and a pretty good supply in some cribs. There was also a fine quantity of dried leaves,[2] which were very acceptable to us ; and without delay we secured them as well as the corn, and then burned the town to ashes ; after which we left the place.

In the field where we gathered the corn we saw plenty of fresh Indian tracks, and we had no doubt they had been scared off by our arrival.

We then went on to meet the main army at the fork road, where I was first to have met Major Gibson. We got that evening as far back as the encampment we had made the night before we reached the Black Warrior's town, which we had just destroyed. The next day we were entirely out of meat.[3] I went to Col. Coffee, who was then in command of us, and asked his leave to hunt as we marched. He gave me leave, but told me to take mighty good care of myself. I turned aside to hunt, and had not gone far when I found a deer that had just been killed and skinned, and his flesh was still warm and smoking. From this I was sure that the Indian who had killed it had been gone only a very few minutes ; and though I was never much in favour of one hunter stealing from another, yet meat was so scarce in camp, that I thought I must go in for it. So I just took up the deer on my horse before me, and carried it on till night. I could have sold it for almost any price I would have asked; but this wasn't my rule, neither in peace nor war. Whenever I had any thing, and saw a fellow being suffering, I was more anxious to relieve him than to benefit myself. And this is one of the true secrets of my being a poor man to this day.[4] But it is my way; and while it has often left me with an empty purse, which is as near the devil as any thing else I have seen, yet it has never left my heart empty of consolations which money couldn't buy,—the consolations of having sometimes fed the hungry and covered the naked.

I gave all my deer away, except a small part I kept for myself, and just sufficient to make a good supper for my mess;[5] for meat was getting to be a rarity to us all. We had to live mostly on parched corn. The next day we marched on, and at night took up camp near a large cane brake. While here, I told my mess I would again try for some meat; so I took my rifle and cut out, but hadn't gone far, when I discovered a large gang of hogs. I shot one of them down in his tracks, and the rest broke directly towards the camp. In a few minutes, the guns began to roar, as bad as if the whole army had been in an In-

H

4. There is no question of that; see his letters to his son, Jan. 10, 1834 (L.C.), and to Margaret and Wiley Flowers, Jan. 9, 1836.

5. Those with whom he messed or ate.

dian battle ; and the hogs to squeal as bad as the pig did, when the devil turned barber.[6] I shouldered my hog, and went on to the camp ; and when I got there I found they had killed a good many of the hogs, and a fine fat cow into the bargain, that had broke out of the cane brake. We did very well that night, and the next morning marched on to a Cherokee town, where our officers stop'd, and gave the inhabitants an order on Uncle Sam for their cow, and the hogs we had killed. The next day we met the main army, having had, as we thought, hard times, and a plenty of them, though we had yet seen hardly the beginning of trouble.

After our meeting we went on to Radcliff's, where I had been before while out as a spy ;[7] and when we got there, we found he had hid all his provisions. We also got into the secret, that he was the very rascal who had sent the runner to the Indian camp, with the news that the "red sticks" were crossing at the Ten Islands ; and that his object was to scare me and my men away, and send us back with a false alarm.[8]

To make some atonement for this, we took the old scroundrell's two big sons with us, and made them serve in the war.

We then marched to a place, which we called

Camp Mills ;[9] and here it was that Captain Cannon was promoted to a colonel, and Colonel Coffee to a general. We then marched to the Ten Islands, on the Coosa river, where we established a fort ; and our spy companies were sent out. They soon made prisoners of Bob Catala and his warriors, and, in a few days afterwards, we heard of some Indians in a town about eight miles off.[10] So we mounted our horses, and put out for that town, under the direction of two friendly Creeks we had taken for pilots. We had also a Cherokee colonel, Dick Brown, and some of his men with us. When we got near the town we divided ; one of our pilots going with each division. And so we passed on each side of the town, keeping near to it, until our lines met on the far side. We then closed up at both ends, so as to surround it completely ; and then we sent Captain Hammond's company of rangers to bring on the affray.[11] He had advanced near the town, when the Indians saw him, and they raised the yell, and came running at him like so many red devils. The main army was now formed in a hollow square around the town, and they pursued Hammond till they came in reach of us. We then gave them a fire, and they returned it, and then ran back into their town. We began to close on

9. Camp Wells, which was evidently somewhere between Tuscaloosa and Gadsden. Waldo, *Memoirs,* 70–71.

10. The town was Tallusahatchee.

11. Crockett's account, in most cases, agrees with the official reports from Coffee to Jackson, Nov. 4, 1813, and Jackson to Gov. Willie Blount of the same date. Waldo, *Memoirs,* 70–75.

12. Isaiah 4:1—"And in that day [of calamities for Judah and punishment of women for pride] seven women shall take hold of one man, saying, We will eat our own bread, and wear our own apparel: only let us be called by thy name, to take away our reproach."

13. According to Jackson's report, no officer was killed, but he may have died later of his wound. The incident, as described by Crockett, is not included in the official reports.

the town by making our files closer and closer, and the Indians soon saw they were our property. So most of them wanted us to take them prisoners ; and their squaws and all would run and take hold of any of us they could, and give themselves up. I saw seven squaws have hold of one man, which made me think of the Scriptures. So I hollered out the Scriptures was fulfilling ; that there was seven women holding to one man's coat tail.[12] But I believe it was a hunting-shirt all the time. We took them all prisoners that came out to us in this way ; but I saw some warriors run into a house, until I counted forty-six of them. We pursued them until we got near the house, when we saw a squaw sitting in the door, and she placed her feet against the bow she had in her hand, and then took an arrow, and, raising her feet, she drew with all her might, and let fly at us, and she killed a man, whose name, I believe, was Moore. He was a lieutenant,[13] and his death so enraged us all, that she was fired on, and had at least twenty balls blown through her. This was the first man I ever saw killed with a bow and arrow. We now shot them like dogs ; and then set the house on fire, and burned it up with the forty-six warriors in it. I recollect seeing a boy who was shot down near the house. His arm and thigh was broken, and he was so near the burning house that the grease was stewing out of him. In this situation he was still trying to crawl along; but not a murmur escaped him, though he was only about twelve years old. So sullen is the Indian, when his dander is up, that he had sooner die than make a noise, or ask for quarters.[14]

The number that we took prisoners, being added to the number we killed, amounted to one hundred and eighty-six;[15] though I don't remember the exact number of either. We had five of our men killed. We then returned to our camp, at which our fort was erected, and known by the name of Fort Strother.[16] No provisions had yet reached us, and we had now been for several days on half rations. However we went back to our Indian town on the next day,[17] when many of the carcasses of the Indians were still to be seen. They looked very awful, for the burning had not entirely consumed them, but given them a very terrible appearance, at least what remained of them. It was, somehow or other, found out that the house had a potatoe cellar under it, and an immediate examination was made, for we were all as hungry as wolves. We found a fine chance of potatoes in it, and hunger compel-

H 2

14. Crockett's complete lack of sympathy—not at the time of the battle, but at the retelling in 1834—makes one suspicious of the speech on behalf of the Indians which he supposedly made in Congress in 1830.

15. This is probably a loose reading of the official report. The 80 prisoners were in addition to the 186 killed. Jackson commented: "We have retaliated for the destruction of Fort Mims." Waldo, *Memoirs*, 71–75.

16. As Jackson extended his line into Indian territory, he consolidated his rear, building forts or strong points to insure his lines of supply and communication. The first fort built by Jackson south of the Tennessee River was Fort Deposit, at the tip of the deep south bend of the Tennessee River, southeast of Huntsville. From this point he moved straight across the mountains to Gadsden and the Ten Islands and then proceeded on down the Coosa River toward Montgomery and the Indians' stronghold, the Hickory Ground, to establish other lines.

17. This would be Nov. 4, 1813. The scarcity of provisions was the one great deterrent to Jackson's quick accomplishment of his objective. Naturally the story which follows is not included in the official reports.

led us to eat them, though I had a little rather not, if I could have helped it, for the oil of the Indians we had burned up on the day before had run down on them, and they looked like they had been stewed with fat meat. We then again returned to the army, and remained there for several days almost starving, as all our beef was gone. We commenced eating the beef-hides, and continued to eat every scrap we could lay our hands on. At length an Indian came to our ground one night, and hollered, and said he wanted to see "Captain Jackson." He was conducted to the general's markee, into which he entered, and in a few minutes we received orders to prepare for marching.

In an hour we were all ready, and took up the line of march. We crossed the Coosa river, and went on in the direction to Fort Taladega.[18] When we arrived near the place, we met eleven hundred painted warriors, the very choice of the Creek nation. They had encamped near the fort, and had informed the friendly Indians who were in it, that if they didn't come out, and fight with them against the whites, they would take their fort and all their ammunition and provision. The friendly party asked three days to consider of it, and agreed that if on the third day they didn't come out

18. Fort Talladega, almost 30 miles due south of Fort Strother. The Coosa River at the Ten Islands runs southwest; Strother was on the northwest side.

ready to fight with them, they might take their fort. Thus they put them off. They then immediately started their runner to General Jackson, and he and the army pushed over, as I have just before stated.[19]

The camp of warriors had their spies out, and discovered us coming, some time before we got to the fort. They then went to the friendly Indians, and told them Captain Jackson was coming, and had a great many fine horses, and blankets, and guns, and every thing else; and if they would come out and help to whip him, and to take his plunder, it should all be divided with those in the fort. They promised that when Jackson came, they would then come out and help to whip him. It was about an hour by sun in the morning, when we got near the fort.[20] We were piloted by friendly Indians, and divided as we had done on a former occasion, so as to go to the right and left of the fort, and, consequently, of the warriors who were camped near it. Our lines marched on, as before, till they met in front, and then closed in the rear, forming again into a hollow square. We then sent on old Major Russell, with his spy company, to bring on the battle; Capt. Evans' company went also.[21] When they got near the fort, the top of it was lined with the friendly Indians, crying

19. The friendly Indians inside the fort were also Creeks. Their chief made his way out in a hogskin disguise, and it was he who was the runner to Jackson. Halbert and Ball, *Creek War*, 269–70.

20. "By sun": after sunrise.

21. Capt. Robert Evans was in command of a company of spies (scouts) under Jackson, Sept. 24, 1813–Feb. 24, 1814. He was mustered out in Davidson County. Creek War Records, envelope 9451.

out as loud as they could roar, "How-dy-do, brother, how-dy-do?" They kept this up till Major Russel had passed by the fort, and was moving on towards the warriors. They were all painted as red as scarlet, and were just as naked as they were born. They had concealed themselves under the bank of a branch, that ran partly around the fort, in the manner of a half moon. Russel was going right into their circle, for he couldn't see them, while the Indians on the top of the fort were trying every plan to show him his danger. But he couldn't understand them. At last, two of them jumped from it, and ran, and took his horse by the bridle, and pointing to where they were, told him there were thousands of them lying under the bank. This brought them to a halt, and about this moment the Indians fired on them, and came rushing forth like a cloud of Egyptian locusts,[22] and screaming like all the young devils had been turned loose, with the old devil of all at their head. Russel's company quit their horses, and took into the fort, and their horses ran up to our line, which was then in full view. The warriors then came yelling on, meeting us, and continued till they were within shot of us, when we fired and killed a considerable number of them. They then broke like a gang of steers, and ran across to our other line, where they were again fired on ; and so we kept them running from one line to the other, constantly under a heavy fire, until we had killed upwards of four hundred of them.[23] They fought with guns, and also with their bows and arrows ; but at length they made their escape through a part of our line, which was made up of drafted militia, which broke ranks, and they passed. We lost fifteen of our men, as brave fellows as ever lived or died. We buried them all in one grave, and started back to our fort ; but before we got there, two more of our men died of wounds they had received ; making our total loss seventeen good fellows in that battle.[24]

We now remained at the fort a few days, but no provision came yet, and we were all likely to perish. The weather also began to get very cold ; and our clothes were nearly worn out, and horses getting very feeble and poor. Our officers proposed to Gen'l. Jackson to let us return home and get fresh horses, and fresh clothing, so as to be better prepared for another campaign ; for our sixty days had long been out, and that was the time we entered for.[25]

But the general took " the responsibility "[26] on himself, and refused. We were, however, determined to go, as I am to put back the deposites, *if*

23. According to Jackson's official report to Gov. Blount, Nov. 15, 1813 (Waldo, *Memoirs*, 82–84), 299 were "left dead on the ground ; no doubt many more were killed who were not found."

24. Crockett's statement that the American loss was 17 is confirmed by Jackson's report. In a letter to Gen. F. L. Claiborne, Dec. 18, 1813 (quoted in Halbert and Ball, *Creek War*, 270), Jackson said: "Could I have followed up that victory [Talladega] immediately, the Creek war, before this, had been terminated. But I was compelled by a double cause, —the want of supplies and the want of co-operation from the East Tennessee troops, to return to this place [Fort Strother]." The war was prolonged by the Hillabee Massacre of Nov. 18. The Hillabee faction of the Creeks had opened negotiations with Jackson for peace, when their towns were attacked by East Tennessee troops under Gen. James White (founder of Knoxville) under orders from Gen. John Cocke, both of whom were apparently unaware of the peace negotiations. The Creeks naturally thought that Jackson had had a hand in a treacherous "doublecross," and all hope of a settlement short of a death struggle was now gone. *Ibid.*, 271–72.

25. Some of the troops' time was expiring, but not Crockett's ; his 90-day enlistment did not end until Dec. 24. Coffee's mounted riflemen, including Crockett were, however, given a furlough to "recruit . . . horses and procure winter clothing." They were then to rendezvous Dec. 8 at Huntsville. Reid and Eaton, *Jackson*, 90.

26. The phrase is the one Jackson employed in moving the deposits while Congress was in adjournment. Because several of the cabinet members had opposed the move, Van Buren suggested that Jack-

son use this phrase in official language to abrogate any compulsion of those cabinet members to resign. Jackson "took the responsibility" on himself to fire the secretary of the treasury (William J. Duane) who would not move the deposits and to replace him by one who would (Roger B. Taney).

27. Washington *Globe* and the "kitchen cabinet." The *Globe*, published by Francis P. Blair, was the administration organ. Blair, in 1834, also published the congressional debates, renamed *Congressional Globe* (formerly *Register of Debates*).

28. Actually, because the mutinous tendency struck first one group and then the other (militia and volunteers), Jackson was able to use the loyal group to restrain the mutiny by the other. Reid and Eaton, *Jackson*, 69–71.

I can. With this, the general issued his orders against it, as he has against the bank. But we began to fix for a start, as provisions were too scarce ; just as Clay, and Webster, and myself are preparing to fix bank matters, on account of the scarcity of money. The general went and placed his cannon on a bridge we had to cross, and ordered out his regulars and drafted men to keep us from crossing ; just as he has planted his Globe and K. C.[27] to alarm the bank men, while his regulars and militia in Congress are to act as artillery men. But when the militia started to guard the bridge, they would holler back to us to bring their knapsacks along when we come, for they wanted to go as bad as we did ;[28] just as many a good fellow now wants his political knapsack brought along, that if, when we come to vote, he sees he has a *fair shake to go*, he may join in and help us to take back the deposites.

We got ready and moved on till we came near the bridge, where the general's men were all strung along on both sides, just like the office-holders are now, to keep us from getting along to the help of the country and the people. But we all had our flints ready picked, and our guns ready primed, that if we were fired on we might fight our way through, or all die together ; just as we are now determined to save the country from ready ruin, or to sink down with it. When we came still nearer the bridge we heard the guards cocking their guns, and we did the same ; just as we have had it in Congress, while the " government" regulars and the people's volunteers have all been setting their political triggers. But, after all, we marched boldly on, and not a gun was fired, nor a life lost ; just as I hope it will be again, that we shall not be afraid of the general's Globe, nor his K. C., nor his regulars, nor their trigger snapping ; but just march boldly over the executive bridge,[29] and take the deposites back where the law placed them, and where they ought to be. When we had passed, no further attempt was made to stop us ; but the general said, we were " the damned'st volunteers he had ever seen in his life ; that we would volunteer and go out and fight, and then at our pleasure would *volunteer* and go home again, in spite of the devil."[30] But we went on ; and near Huntsville we met a reinforcement who were going on to join the army. It consisted of a regiment of volunteers, and was under the command of some one whose name I can't remember. They were sixty-day volunteers.

We got home pretty safely, and in a short time

29. This elaborate figure of the mutiny of the volunteers is patently too fine for Crockett's workmanship and, in addition, is inaccurate. It was Jackson who personally "backed down" the troops at gun point. The troops whose terms of service had expired were soon released when Gov. Blount, because of political considerations, suggested that it would be wise to dismiss them.

30. This is, of course, Crockett's imagination, and his comment below about 60-day volunteers is erroneous.

31. Actually Huntsville. According to Waldo, *Memoirs*, 96, they met there some troops allowed to go home because their terms of service had expired, and they, too, "caught the infection that pervaded the infantry—the fever of private life . . . . Gen. Jackson . . . exerted again his powers [by letter]; but exerted them in vain." Following is the pay-roll record of David Crockett for his first tour of duty, taken from the photostats of the originals, Records of the War of 1812, Vol. 3, Photo 11-C-2(1), pages unnumbered: "David Crockett, private, commenced service September 26, 1813; expiration of service, [19] December 24, 1813; term of service charged, 3 months 6 days. Pay per month $8.00; allowance for pay of horse September, 1813—December 24, 1813, 97 days, $38.80; travelling allowance before muster in and after discharge 120 miles at 25 cents per day, $1.25. Amount of pay, $65.59. Remarks, none." According to these figures, Crockett should have received $65.65, and was short-changed six cents. There is no record in the National Archives that Crockett was back in the army after his discharge on Dec. 24, 1813, until he re-enlisted Sept. 1814. Yet the battles he goes on to describe are the battles of the early part of 1814.

32. According to Reid and Eaton, *Jackson*, 98, some officers and a few privates did respond to Jackson's entreaties and returned to camp. It is possible that Crockett was one of them, if they actually rendezvoused Dec. 8; but if so, he remained only a few weeks—until his term of service expired.

33. On the west bank of the Coosa River.

we had procured fresh horses and a supply of clothing better suited for the season ; and then we returned to Fort Deposite,[31] where our officers held a sort of a *"national convention"* on the subject of a message they had received from General Jackson,—demanding that on our return we should serve out *six months*. We had already served three months instead of two, which was the time we had volunteered for. On the next morning the officers reported to us the conclusions they had come to ; and told us, if any of us felt bound to go on and serve out the six months, we could do so; but that they intended to go back home. I knowed if I went back home I couldn't rest, for I felt it my duty to be out; and when out was, somehow or other, always delighted to be in the very thickest of the danger. A few of us, therefore, determined to push on and join the army. The number I do not recollect, but it was very small.[32]

When we got out there, I joined Major Russel's company of spies. Before we reached the place, General Jackson had started. We went on likewise, and overtook him at a place where we established a fort, called Fort Williams,[33] and leaving men to guard it, we went ahead ; intending to go to a place called the Horse-shoe bend of the Talapoosa river.[34] When we came near that place, we began to find Indian sign plenty, and we struck up camp for the night. About two hours before day, we heard our guard firing, and we were all up in little or no time. We mended up our camp fires, and then fell back in the dark, expecting to see the Indians pouring in; and intending, when they should do so, to shoot them by the light of our own fires. But it happened that they did not rush in as we had expected, but commenced a fire on us as we were. We were encamped in a hollow square, and we not only returned the fire, but continued to shoot as well as we could in the dark, till day broke, when the Indians disappeared. The only guide we had in shooting was to notice the flash of their guns, and then shoot as directly at the place as we could guess.

In this scrape we had four men killed, and several wounded; but whether we killed any of the Indians or not we never could tell, for it is their custom always to carry off their dead, if they can possibly do so. We buried ours, and then made a large log heap over them, and set it on fire, so that the place of their deposite might not be known to the savages, who, we knew, would seek for them, that they might scalp them. We made some horse litters for our wounded, and

I

34. Tallapoosa River. Because Crockett was not present, further documentation has been omitted.

took up a retreat.   We moved on till we came to
a large creek which we had to cross ; and about
half of our men had crossed, when the Indians
commenced firing on our left wing, and they
kept it up very warmly.   We had left Major
Russel and his brother at the camp we had moved
from that morning, to see what discovery they
could make as to the movements of the Indians ;
and about this time, while a warm fire was kept
up on our left, as I have just stated, the major
came up in our rear, and was closely pursued by
a large number of Indians, who immediately
commenced a fire on our artillery men.   They
hid themselves behind a large log, and could kill
one of our men almost every shot, they being in
open ground and exposed.   The worst of all was,
two of our colonels just at this trying moment
left their men, and by *a forced march*, crossed
the creek out of the reach of the fire.   Their
names, at this late day, would do the world no
good, and my object is history alone, and not the
slightest interference with character.   An opportunity was now afforded for Governor Carroll to
distinguish himself, and on this occasion he did
so, by greater bravery than I ever saw any other
man display.   In truth, I believe, as firmly as I
do that General Jackson is president, that if it

hadn't been for Carroll, we should all have been genteely licked that time, for we were in a devil of a fix ; part of our men on one side of the creek, and part on the other, and the Indians all the time pouring it on us, as hot as fresh mustard to a sore shin. I will not say exactly that the old general was whip'd ; but I will say, that if we escaped it at all, it was like old Henry Snider going to heaven, " mit a tam tite squeeze." [35] I think he would confess himself, that he was nearer whip'd this time than he was at any other, for I know that all the world couldn't make him acknowledge that he was *pointedly* whip'd. I know I was mighty glad when it was over, and the savages quit us, for I had begun to think there was one behind every tree in the woods.

We buried our dead, the number of whom I have also forgotten ; and again made horse litters to carry our wounded, and so we put out, and returned to Fort Williams, from which place we had started. [36] In the mean time, my horse had got crippled, and was unfit for service, and as another reinforcement had arrived, I thought they could get along without me for a short time; so I got a furlough and went home, for we had had hard times again on this hunt, and I began to feel as though I had

35. The whole story of Snider, as told in *Life and Adventures*, 79–81, is another of the Dutchman's anecdotes about a miller who was subject to harmless spells of mental derangement when he featured himself to be some great character. More than once the comprehension of an anecdote in the *Narrative* depends upon a prior reading of *Life and Adventures*.

36. They did not stop at Williams, but went all the way to Fort Strother.

37. Site of the decisive battle of the campaign, fought on Mar. 27, 1814. Crockett apparently considered it safe to claim that he was present at the minor engagements, but to claim he was in the famous Battle of Tohopeka (Horseshoe Bend) would have been much too dangerous. Therefore, he conveniently gave himself a furlough to explain his absence. At the time of his real furlough earlier, he represented himself falsely as "absent without leave."

done Indian fighting enough for one time. I remained at home until after the army had returned to the Horse-shoe bend, and fought the battle there.[37] But not being with them at that time, of course no history of that fight can be expected of me.

CHAPTER VII.

Soon after this,[1] an army was to be raised to go to Pensacola, and I determined to go again with them, for I wanted a small taste of British fighting, and I supposed they would be there.

Here again the entreaties of my wife were thrown in the way of my going, but all in vain; for I always had a way of just going ahead, at whatever I had a mind to. One of my neighbours, hearing I had determined to go, came to me, and offered me a hundred dollars to go in his place as a substitute, as he had been drafted. I told him I was better raised than to hire myself out to be shot at ;[2] but that I would go, and he should go too, and in that way the government would have the services of us both. But we didn't call General Jackson "the government" in those days, though we used to go and fight under him in the war.

I fixed up, and joined old Major Russel again ;[3] but we couldn't start with the main army, but

I 2

1. He probably means soon after the Battle of Horseshoe Bend. Actually, it was about six months later.

2. Not better raised than to hire somebody else to do the same thing, however, as he tells us later he did for the last month of this tour of duty.

3. Creek War Records show: "Mounted Gunmen, September 28, 1814, Mustered; discharged March 27, 1815, David Crockett, rank 3rd Sergeant. Enlisted September 28, 1814—March 27, 1815." Records of the War of 1812, Vol. VIII, photo 7-C-2(2). His name is also on the Pay Roll Record: "Time, 6 months, 2 days. Pay, rate $11.00 per month. Amount of pay $66.70."

4. He does not mean Ditto's Landing where he had crossed it the first time, but where he had crossed it later, at Kelton's Bluff during the first enlistment.

5. The Choctaw and Chickasaw nations occupied much of the present state of Mississippi.

6. According to Crockett, they crossed at about present-day Florence, Ala., then marched due south near the western boundary to a point a few miles north of Mobile and the Gulf, where Fort St. Stephens was located. This was north of the Cut-off, where a large island, the Nannahubba, is formed near present Jackson, Miss. Fort Mims was at the junction of the two rivers, but on the east side of the Alabama River. Pensacola is due southeast of this position. Halbert and Ball, *Creek War*, 29, 107–108.

7. After their defeat some of the Creeks fled to Pensacola, where they were used by the British in their movements against Mobile and New Orleans. Jackson, now major general in the U. S. Army and commander of the 7th Military District, marched to the defense of Mobile and then moved against Pensacola. Halbert and Ball, *Creek War*, 279–84.

followed on, in a little time, after them. In a day or two, we had a hundred and thirty men in our company; and we went over and crossed the Muscle Shoals at the same place where I had crossed when first out,[4] and where we burned the Black Warriors' town. We passed through the Choctaw and Chickesaw nations,[5] on to Fort Stephens, and from thence to what is called the Cut-off, at the junction of the Tom-Bigby with the Alabama river. This place is near the old Fort Mimms, where the Indians committed the great butchery at the commencement of the war.[6]

We were here about two days behind the main army, who had left their horses at the Cut-off, and taken it on foot; and they did this because there was no chance for forage between there and Pensacola.[7] We did the same, leaving men enough to take care of our horses, and cut out on foot for that place. It was about eighty miles off; but in good heart we shouldered our guns, blankets, and provisions, and trudged merrily on. About twelve o'clock the second day, we reached the encampment of the main army, which was situated on a hill, overlooking the city of Pensacola. My commander, Major Russel, was a great favourite with Gen'l. Jackson, and our arrival was hailed with great applause, though we were a little after the feast ; for they had taken the town and fort before we got there.[8] That evening we went down into the town, and could see the British fleet lying in sight of the place. We got some liquor, and took a " horn" or so, and went back to the camp. We remained there that night, and in the morning we marched back towards the Cut-off. We pursued this direction till we reached old Fort Mimms, where we remained two or three days. It was here that Major Russel was promoted from his command, which was only that of a captain of spies, to the command of a major in the line.[9] He had been known long before at home as old Major Russel, and so we all continued to call him in the army. A Major Childs,[10] from East Tennessee, also commanded a battalion, and his and the one Russel was now appointed to command, composed a regiment, which, by agreement with General Jackson, was to quit his army and go to the south, to kill up the Indians on the Seamby river.[11]

General Jackson and the main army set out the next morning for New Orleans, and a Colonel Blue[12] took command of the regiment which I have before described. We remained, however, a few days after the general's departure, and then started also on our route.

8. Jackson took Pensacola Nov. 7, 1814, after only a token resistance. He was preparing to storm Fort Barrancas on the morning of the eighth when it was blown up in breach of the previous day's treaty, and Jackson decided to withdraw his troops. "But before I did," says his report, "I had the pleasure to see the British depart." This was on Nov. 9, and since Crockett says he saw the English ships, he must have arrived about noon Nov. 8. On the ninth the troops started back for Fort Mims. Jackson's Nov. 14 report, written from the Tensaw River (he was on his way to Mobile), includes a statement that "a part [750] of the Choctaws were led by Maj. [Uriah] Blue, of the 39th, and Maj. Kennedy, of Mississippi Territory." Waldo, *Memoirs*, 170–76.

9. Since Maj. Russell was the commander of the battalion before it was discharged, it was known as his battalion on the records for the whole muster period, Sept. 28, 1814, to Mar. 27, 1815. Crockett is likely correct, however, that it was not until about mid-November that Capt. Russell was promoted to major. Creek War Records, envelope 9444.

10. "Maj. Childs Batt'n Tennessee Mounted Volunteers in Brig. Gen. Coffee's Brigade under Maj. Gen. Jackson, from Sept. 20, 1814 to May 1, 1815. Certified Knox County Muster Role [Roll], May 1st 1815, signed John Childs, Major." *Ibid*.

11. The Escambia River empties into Pensacola Bay. The Indians whom the British had been training took to the swamps, and it was necessary to try to drive them out or, at any rate, to set up a rearguard action. For the remainder of his War of 1812 service, Crockett was detached to help run out the remaining Creeks from the swamps. Two battalions, one under Childs, one under Russell, and both under Blue, were in the detachment. Jackson went on to Mobile and then to New Orleans and glory.

12. Maj. Uriah Blue. Since his duties gave him

superior authority over the majors of the Volunteers, it would seem that he should have been a colonel, which perhaps may explain Crockett's error. Bassett, *Jackson*, I, 143, says: "Major Blue of the 39th regiment, was given command of the force intended to operate against the Indians . . . along the Escambia."

As it gave rise to so much war and bloodshed, it may not be improper here to give a little description of Fort Mimms, and the manner in which the Indian war commenced. The fort was built right in the middle of a large old field, and in it the people had been forted so long and so quietly, that they didn't apprehend any danger at all, and had, therefore, become quite careless. A small negro boy, whose business it was to bring up the calves at milking time, had been out for that purpose, and on coming back, he said he saw a great many Indians. At this the inhabitants took the alarm, and closed their gates and placed out their guards, which they continued for a few days. But finding that no attack was made, they concluded the little negro had lied; and again threw their gates open, and set all their hands out to work their fields. The same boy was out again on the same errand, when, returning in great haste and alarm, he informed them that he had seen the Indians as thick as trees in the woods. He was not believed, but was tucked up to receive a flogging for the supposed lie; and was actually getting badly licked at the very moment when the Indians came in a troop, loaded with rails, with which they stop'd all the port-holes of the fort on one side except the bastion; and then they fell in to cutting down the picketing. Those inside the fort had only the bastion to shoot from, as all the other holes were spiked up; and they shot several of the Indians, while engaged in cutting. But as fast as one would fall, another would seize up the axe and chop away, until they succeeded in cutting down enough of the picketing to admit them to enter. They then began to rush through, and continued until they were all in. They immediately commenced scalping, without regard to age or sex ; having forced the inhabitants up to one side of the fort, where they carried on the work of death as a butcher would in a slaughter pen.[13]

The scene was particularly described to me by a young man who was in the fort when it happened, and subsequently went on with us to Pensacola. He said that he saw his father, and mother, his four sisters, and the same number of brothers, all butchered in the most shocking manner, and that he made his escape by running over the heads[14] of the crowd, who were against the fort wall, to the top of the fort, and then jumping off, and taking to the woods. He was closely pursued by several Indians, until he came to a small byo,[15] across which there was a log. He knew the log was hollow on the under side, so he slip'd under

13. For an excellent account of this massacre, see Halbert and Ball, *Creek War,* 143–76. After the Battle of Burnt Corn, inhabitants on Tensaw and along Little River gathered around the residence of Samuel Mims, an old Indian, and built an almost square stockade. In Aug. 1813, 553 people were within—about 265 soldiers and the remainder children (100), women, noncombatants, and Negro servants (100). Of the soldiers 175 were Mississippi Volunteers under Maj. Daniel Beasley, whose dereliction, in refusing to permit measures for defense and ignoring warnings, was mainly responsible for the disaster. Ironically, when the attack occurred, Beasley was the first to fall, when he "tried to shut the sandbarred gate." After a carnage of about two or three hours, the Indians withdrew, only to return shortly afterwards. The gates had now been closed. The Indians then set fire to the buildings by means of arrows, and those inside still alive crowded into what they called the bastion. They were, however, a prey to those who attacked them. When the Indians left about five o'clock, all inside were dead and most so mutilated as not to be identifiable. *Ibid.,* 151–56.

14. This was entirely possible according to the accounts. Exactly how many escaped is not known —perhaps 50 or 75 survived. Lt. W. R. Chambliss ran out of the stockade at the height of the onslaught to a log heap for refuge, and the Indians did not notice him. The Indians later set it afire, but just as the smoke and heat became unbearable, something called the Indians away, and he escaped. *Ibid.,* 161. Of all the accounts of escapes, this seems nearest to the story told by Crockett.

15. Bayou.

16. Fort Montgomery, a mile or two north of the destroyed Fort Mims, was a new one, erected by Col. Thomas H. Benton. *Ibid.*, 280.

17. Going south, they turned east toward Florida.

the log and hid himself. He said he heard the Indians walk over him several times back and forward. He remained, nevertheless, still till night, when he came out, and finished his escape. The name of this young man has entirely escaped my recollection, though his tale greatly excited my feelings. But to return to my subject. The regiment marched from where Gen'l. Jackson had left us to Fort Montgomery, which was distant from Fort Mimms about a mile and a half, and there we remained for some days.[16]

Here we supplied ourselves pretty well with beef, by killing wild cattle which had formerly belonged to the people who perished in the fort, but had gone wild after their massacre.

When we marched from Fort Montgomery, we went some distance back towards Pensacola ; then we turned to the left,[17] and passed through a poor piny country, till we reached the Scamby river, near which we encamped. We had about one thousand men, and as a part of that number, one hundred and eighty-six Chickesaw and Choctaw Indians with us. That evening a boat landed from Pensacola, bringing many articles that were both good and necessary ; such as sugar and coffee, and liquors of all kinds. The same evening, the Indians we had along proposed to cross the river, and the officers thinking it might be well for them to do so, consented ; and Major Russell went with them, taking sixteen white men, of which number I was one. We camped on the opposite bank that night, and early in the morning we set out. We had not gone far before we came to a place where the whole country was covered with water, and looked like a sea. We didn't stop for this, tho', but just put in like so many spaniels, and waded on, sometimes up to our armpits, until we reached the pine hills, which made our distance through the water about a mile and a half. Here we struck up a fire to warm ourselves, for it was cold, and we were chilled through by being so long in the water. We again moved on, keeping our spies out ; two to our left near the bank of the river, two straight before us, and two others on our right. We had gone in this way about six miles up the river, when our spies on the left came to us leaping the brush like so many old bucks, and informed us that they had discovered a camp of Creek Indians, and that we must kill them. Here we paused for a few minutes, and the prophets pow-wowed over their men awhile, and then got out their paint, and painted them, all according to their custom when going into battle. They then brought their paint to old Major Russell, and said

to him, that as he was an officer, he must be painted too.   He agreed, and they painted him just as
they had done themselves.   We let the Indians
understand that we white men would first fire on
the camp, and then fall back, so as to give the Indians a chance to rush in and scalp them.   The
Chickasaws marched on our left hand, and the
Choctaws on our right, and we moved on till we
got in hearing of the camp, where the Indians
were employed in beating up what they called
chainy briar root.   On this they mostly subsisted.   On a nearer approach we found they were
on an island, and that we could get to them.
While we were chatting about this matter, we
heard some guns fired, and in a very short time
after a keen whoop, which satisfied us, that whereever it was, there was war on a small scale.   With
that we all broke, like quarter horses, for the
firing ; and when we got there we found it was
our two front spies, who related to us the following
story :—As they were moving on, they had met
with two Creeks who were out hunting their
horses ; as they approached each other, there was a
large cluster of green bay bushes exactly between
them, so that they were within a few feet of meeting before either was discovered.   Our spies
walked up to them, and speaking in the Shawnee

tongue, informed them that General Jackson was at Pensacola, and they were making their escape, and wanted to know where they could get something to eat. The Creeks told them that nine miles up the Conaker,[18] the river they were then on, there was a large camp of Creeks, and they had cattle and plenty to eat; and further, that their own camp was on an island about a mile off, and just below the mouth of the Conaker. They held their conversation and struck up a fire, and smoked together, and shook hands, and parted. One of the Creeks had a gun, the other had none; and as soon as they had parted, our Choctaws turned round and shot down the one that had the gun, and the other attempted to run off. They snapped several times at him, but the gun still missing fire, they took after him, and overtaking him, one of them struck him over the head with his gun, and followed up his blows till he killed him.

The gun was broken in the combat, and they then fired off the gun of the Creek they had killed, and raised the war-whoop. When we reached them, they had cut off the heads of both the Indians; and each of those Indians with us would walk up to one of the heads, and taking his war club would strike on it. This was done by every one of them; and when they had got done, I took

K

18. Conecuh River, which joins the Escambia near the northern boundary of Florida, due north of Pensacola.

one of their clubs, and walked up as they had done, and struck it on the head also. At this they all gathered round me, and patting me on the shoulder, would call me " Warrior—warrior."

They scalped the heads, and then we moved on a short distance to where we found a trace leading in towards the river. We took this trace and pursued it, till we came to where a Spaniard had been killed and scalped, together with a woman, who we supposed to be his wife, and also four children. I began to feel mighty ticklish along about this time, for I knowed if there was no danger then, there had been ; and I felt exactly like there still was. We, however, went on till we struck the river, and then continued down it till we came opposite to the Indian camp, where we found they were still beating their roots.

It was now late in the evening, and they were in a thick cane brake. We had some few friendly Creeks with us, who said they could decoy them. So we all hid behind trees and logs, while the attempt was made. The Indians would not agree that we should fire, but pick'd out some of their best gunners, and placed them near the river. Our Creeks went down to the river's side, and hailed the camp in the Creek language. We heard an answer, and an Indian man started down towards the river, but didn't come in sight. He went back and again commenced beating his roots, and sent a squaw. She came down, and talked with our Creeks until dark came on. They told her they wanted her to bring them a canoe. To which she replied, that their canoe was on our side ; that two of their men had gone out to hunt their horses and hadn't yet returned. They were the same two we had killed. The canoe was found, and forty of our picked Indian warriors were crossed over to take the camp. There was at last only one man in it, and he escaped ; and they took two squaws, and ten children, but killed none of them, of course.

We had run nearly out of provisions, and Major Russell had determined to go up the Conaker to the camp we had heard of from the Indians we had killed. I was one that he selected to go down the river that night for provisions, with the canoe, to where we had left our regiment. I took with me a man by the name of John Guess, and one of the friendly Creeks, and cut out. It was very dark, and the river was so full that it overflowed the banks and the adjacent low bottoms. This rendered it very difficult to keep the channel, and particularly as the river was very crooked. At about ten o'clock at night we reached the camp,

19. Capt. William Russell, of Tennessee Mounted Gunmen, was mustered in Sept. 28, 1814, at Fayetteville, Tenn., and discharged Mar. 27, 1815; was mustered in again, June 15, 1815, at Murfreesboro. Creek War Records, envelope 9425. Capt. John Trimble of the East Tennessee Mounted Volunteer Gunmen was mustered in Jan. 20, 1814, and out May 20, 1814, in Blount County, certified in Knox County. *Ibid.*, envelope 9428. Later he was in a battalion commanded by Russell in Gen. Coffee's brigade, serving from Oct. 5, 1814, to Apr. 5, 1815. *Ibid.*, envelope 9425.

and were to return by morning to Major Russell, with provisions for his trip up the river ; but on informing Colonel Blue of this arrangement, he vetoed it as quick as General Jackson did the bank bill ; and said, if Major Russell didn't come back the next day, it would be bad times for him. I found we were not to go up the Conaker to the Indian camp, and a man of my company offered to go up in my place to inform Major Russell. I let him go ; and they reached the major, as I was told, about sunrise in the morning, who immediately returned with those who were with him to the regiment, and joined us where we crossed the river, as hereafter stated.

The next morning we all fixed up, and marched down the Scamby to a place called Miller's Landing, where we swam our horses across, and sent on two companies down on the side of the bay opposite to Pensacola, where the Indians had fled when the main army first marched to that place. One was the company of Captain William Russell, a son of the old major, and the other was commanded by a Captain Trimble.[19] They went on, and had a little skirmish with the Indians. They killed some, and took all the balance prisoners, though I don't remember the numbers. We again met those companies in a day or two, and sent the prisoners they had taken on to Fort Montgomery, in charge of some of our Indians.

I did hear, that after they left us, the Indians killed and scalped all the prisoners,[20] and I never heard the report contradicted.   I cannot positively say it was true, but I think it entirely probable, for it is very much like the Indian character.

K 2

20. Since, according to *Niles' Weekly Register*, VIII, 41 (Mar. 18, 1815), "Major Blue lately went on an expedition from Mobile against the Creek indians, and has returned with 170 Tallapoosa prisoners," perhaps all of those sent back were not then scalped, for Blue later had some to pick up at the forts to take back.

CHAPTER VIII.

WHEN we made a move from the point where we met the companies, we set out for Chatahachy, the place for which we had started when we left Fort Montgomery.[1] At the start we had taken only twenty days' rations of flour, and eight days' rations of beef ; and it was now thirty-four days before we reached that place. We were, therefore, in extreme suffering for want of something to eat, and exhausted with our exposure and the fatigues of our journey. I remember well, that I had not myself tasted bread but twice in nineteen days. I had bought a pretty good supply of coffee from the boat that had reached us from Pensacola, on the Scamby, and on that we chiefly subsisted. At length, one night our spies came in, and informed us they had found Holm's village on the Chatahachy river ; and we made an immediate push for that place. We traveled all night, expecting to get something to eat when we got there. We arrived about sunrise, and near the

1. Probably about Jan. 1, 1815. Shackford, *Crockett*, 30. Crockett probably refers to the Chattahoochee River, the lower extremity of which is now known as the Apalachicola. The ration situation which Crockett describes below is not exaggerated. Political rivalries in the army and in the government, added to normal inertia and inefficiency, starved the supply lines.

2. Not Jackson himself; he did not return to Nashville until May 15. Bassett, *Correspondence*, II, 112,
204. Even Gen. Coffee, of his army, en route home,
wrote a letter to his wife from "near Natchez," Mar.
26, 1815. *Tennessee Historical Magazine* 2 (Dec.
1916), 295.

3. The fort lay in the line of march between their
position in Florida and Fort Strother to which they
were traveling. Men were sent with Russell to get
food, while the remainder of the troops followed
along the same route.

place prepared for battle. We were all so furious,
that even the certainty of a pretty hard fight
could not have restrained us. We made a furious
charge on the town, but to our great mortification
and surprise, there wasn't a human being in it.
The Indians had all run off and left it. We
burned the town, however; but, melancholy to
tell, we found no provision whatever. We then
turned about, and went back to the camp we had
left the night before, as nearly starved as any set
of poor fellows ever were in the world.

We staid there only a little while, when we
divided our regiment; and Major Childs, with
his men, went back the way we had come for a
considerable distance, and then turned to Baton-
Rouge, where they joined General Jackson and
the main army on their return from Orleans.[2]
Major Russell and his men struck for Fort Decatur,
on the Talapoosa river.[3] Some of our friendly
Indians, who knew the country, went on ahead of
us, as we had no trail except the one they made
to follow. With them we sent some of our ablest
horses and men, to get us some provisions, to prevent us from absolutely starving to death. As
the army marched, I hunted every day, and would
kill every hawk, bird, and squirrel that I could
find. Others did the same; and it was a rule

with us, that when we stop'd at night, the hunters would throw all they killed in a pile, and then we would make a general division among all the men. One evening I came in, having killed nothing that day. I had a very sick man in my mess, and I wanted something for him to eat, even if I starved myself. So I went to the fire of a Captain Cowen,[4] who commanded my company after the promotion of Major Russell, and informed him that I was on the hunt of something for a sick man to eat. I knowed the captain was as bad off as the rest of us, but I found him broiling a turkey's gizzard. He said he had divided the turkey out among the sick, that Major Smiley[5] had killed it, and that nothing else had been killed that day. I immediately went to Smiley's fire, where I found him broiling another gizzard. I told him, that it was the first turkey I had ever seen have two gizzards. But so it was, I got nothing for my sick man. And now seeing that every fellow must shift for himself, I determined that in the morning, I would come up missing; so I took my mess and cut out to go ahead of the army. We know'd that nothing more could happen to us if we went than if we staid, for it looked like it was to be starvation any way; we therefore determined to go on the old saying,

4. See Creek War Records, envelope 9425, for muster roll of Capt. John Cowan's company, including the name of David Crockett, as 3rd sergeant, though Crockett does not tell us anywhere of his rank on this tour.

5. No record of a Maj. Smiley appears among the Tennessee Volunteers; perhaps he was with the Mississippi Dragoons.

6. The origin of this phrase is attributed to Crockett not only in the *Dictionary of American English* but also in Charles E. Funk, *A Hog on Ice and Other Curious Expressions* (New York, 1948), 36.

7. If they were traveling towards the Tallapoosa River, as they must have been since they were following in the wake of those going to Fort Decatur, Crockett must be mistaken, for the Escambia lay far to their left, which was west. It is more likely that the reference is to the Choctawhatchee near its head, or one of its tributaries.

root hog or die.[6] We passed two camps, at which our men, that had gone on before us, had killed Indians. At one they had killed nine, and at the other three. About daylight we came to a small river, which I thought was the Scamby;[7] but we continued on for three days, killing little or nothing to eat; till, at last, we all began to get nearly ready to give up the ghost, and lie down and die; for we had no prospect of provision, and we knew we couldn't go much further without it.

We came to a large prairie, that was about six miles across it, and in this I saw a trail which I knowed was made by bear, deer, and turkeys. We went on through it till we came to a large creek, and the low grounds were all set over with wild rye, looking as green as a wheat field. We here made a halt, unsaddled our horses, and turned them loose to graze.

One of my companions, a Mr. Vanzant, and myself, then went up the low grounds to hunt. We had gone some distance, finding nothing; when at last, I found a squirrel; which I shot, but he got into a hole in the tree. The game was small, but necessity is not very particular; so I thought I must have him, and I climbed that tree thirty feet high, without a limb, and pulled him out of his hole. I shouldn't relate such small matters, only to show what lengths a hungry man will go to, to get something to eat. I soon killed two other squirrels, and fired at a large hawk. At this a large gang of turkeys rose from the cane brake, and flew across the creek to where my friend was, who had just before crossed it. He soon fired on a large gobler, and I heard it fall. By this time my gun was loaded again, and I saw one sitting on my side of the creek, which had flew over when he fired; so I blazed away, and down I brought him. I gathered him up, and a fine turkey he was. I now began to think we had struck a breeze of luck, and almost forgot our past sufferings, in the prospect of once more having something to eat. I raised the shout, and my comrade came to me, and we went on to our camp with the game we had killed. While we were gone, two of our mess had been out, and each of them had found a bee tree. We turned into cooking some of our game, but we had neither salt nor bread. Just at this moment, on looking down the creek, we saw our men, who had gone on before us for provisions, coming to us. They came up, and measured out to each man a cupfull of flower. With this, we thickened our soup, when our turkey was cooked, and our friends took dinner with us, and then went on.[8]

8. Crockett and his "mess" had gone on in front of the main body of troops. This returning detachment continued on back toward the main body, after a turkey dinner.

We now took our tomahawks, and went and cut our bee-trees, out of which we got a fine chance of honey; though we had been starving so long that we feared to eat much at a time, till, like the Irish by hanging, we got used to it again. We rested that night without moving our camp; and the next morning myself and Vanzant again turned out to hunt. We had not gone far, before I wounded a fine buck very badly; and while pursuing him, I was walking on a large tree that had fallen down, when from the top of it, a large bear broke out and ran off. I had no dogs, and I was sorry enough for it; for of all the hunting I ever did, I have always delighted most in bear hunting. Soon after this, I killed a large buck; and we had just gotten him to camp, when our poor starved army came up. They told us, that to lessen their sufferings as much as possible, Captain William Russell had had his horse led up to be shot for them to eat, just at the moment that they saw our men returning, who had carried on the flour.

We were now about fourteen miles from Fort Decatur, and we gave away all our meat, and honey,[9]and went on with the rest of the army. When we got there, they could give us only one ration of meat, but not a mouthful of bread. I immediately got a canoe, and taking my gun, crossed

9. Gave it away to others in the army, thinking that food would be plentiful at Fort Decatur.

over the river, and went to the Big Warrior's town.[10] I had a large hat, and I offered an Indian a silver dollar for my hat full of corn. He told me that his corn was all "*shuestea*," which in English means, it was all gone. But he showed me where an Indian lived, who, he said, had corn. I went to him, and made the same offer. He could talk a little broken English, and said to me, "You got any powder? You got bullet?" I told him I had. He then said, "Me swap my corn, for powder and bullet." I took out about ten bullets, and showed him; and he proposed to give me a hat full of corn for them. I took him up, mighty quick. I then offered to give him ten charges of powder for another hat full of corn. To this he agreed very willingly. So I took off my hunting-shirt, and tied up my corn; and though it had cost me very little of my powder and lead, yet I wouldn't have taken fifty silver dollars for it. I returned to the camp, and the next morning we started for the Hickory Ground, which was thirty miles off. It was here that General Jackson met the Indians, and made peace with the body of the nation.[11]

We got nothing to eat at this place, and we had yet to go forty-nine miles, over a rough and wilderness country, to Fort Williams. Parched corn, and but little even of that, was our daily subsist-

L

10. Not to be confused with Black Warrior's town at the site of Tuscaloosa, far to the west; Big Warrior's town was above Montgomery on the Tallapoosa. They were now back among the friendly Creeks, or at any rate among those who had agreed to the treaty and were not at war.

11. In the treaty signed Aug. 9, 1814, the Creeks had ceded to the U.S. all of that territory beginning just above Fort Jackson (at Hickory Ground, near the confluence of the Coosa and Tallapoosa rivers) and extending almost to Fort Armstrong—in other words, from a point just north of Montgomery, Ala., to a point about as far north as Rome, Ga., above Gadsden, Ala. The troops, therefore, were almost back into territory owned by the U.S. The troops were crossing now from the Tallapoosa to the Coosa, just above Montgomery. Thereafter they went up the Coosa north, via Fort Williams and Fort Talladega, to Fort Strother. There they turned northwest, crossed the mountains to Ditto's Landing and Huntsville, and so returned to their point of departure, which in Crockett's case was Bean's Creek, about 10 miles south of Winchester, Tenn.

ence. When we reached Fort Williams, we got one ration of pork and one of flour, which was our only hope until we could reach Fort Strother.

The horses were now giving out, and I remember to have seen thirteen good horses left in one day, the saddles and bridles being thrown away. It was thirty-nine miles to Fort Strother, and we had to pass directly by Fort Talladego, where we first had the big Indian battle with the eleven hundred painted warriors. We went through the old battle ground, and it looked like a great gourd patch; the sculls of the Indians who were killed still lay scattered all about, and many of their frames were still perfect, as the bones had not separated. But about five miles before we got to this battle ground, I struck a trail, which I followed until it led me to one of their towns. Here I swap'd some more of my powder and bullets for a little corn.

I pursued on, by myself, till some time after night, when I came up with the rest of the army. That night my company and myself did pretty well, as I divided out my corn among them. The next morning we met the East Tennessee troops, who were on their road to Mobile, and my youngest brother was with them.[12] They had plenty of corn and provisions, and they gave me what I wanted for myself and my horse. I remained

12. The East Tennessee troops were new recruits for trouble with the British on the coast. Crockett's youngest brother was named Joseph, according to Torrence, *Crockett*, 4. Crockett speaks of him again at the beginning of ch. IX. The date here may be February instead of March (when his tour expired), for Crockett later says that for the last few weeks of his tour he paid a substitute to perform for him; there is no mention of this, however, in the official records.

with them that night, though my company went across the Coosa river to the fort,[13] where they also had the good fortune to find plenty of provisions. Next morning, I took leave of my brother and all my old neighbours, for there were a good many of them with him, and crossed over to my men at the fort. Here I had enough to go on, and after remaining a few days, cut out for home. Nothing more, worthy of the reader's attention, transpired till I was safely landed at home once more with my wife and children.[14] I found them all well and doing well; and though I was only a rough sort of a backwoodsman, they seemed mighty glad to see me, however little the quality folks might suppose it. For I do reckon we love as hard in the backwood country, as any people in the whole creation.

But I had been home only a few days, when we received orders to start again, and go on to the Black Warrior and Cahawba rivers, to see if there was no Indians there.[15] I know'd well enough there was none, and I wasn't willing to trust my craw any more where there was neither any fighting to do, nor any thing to go on; and so I agreed to give a young man, who wanted to go, the balance of my wages if he would serve out my time, which was about a month. He did so, and when they returned,

13. Fort Strother.

14. Note that Crockett says his wife was alive and well at the time of his return, which cannot have been prior to Feb. 1815. *Life and Adventures* said she died while he was at war and that he had to come home to the children for that reason.

15. In west central Alabama, between Tuscaloosa and Selma. The Cahaba River parallels the Black Warrior to the east and flows into the Alabama River a few miles below Selma.

16. An expression which had by now been closely identified with Crockett's name by the journalists of the East.

17. There was another David Crockett (probably a relative) in the Creek War, in the company of Capt. James McFerrin under Col. William Pillow. While previously serving under Col. Thomas H. Benton, this Crockett deserted on Nov. 19, 1813, during his period of enlistment, Sept. 26, 1813, to Dec. 10, 1813. Records of the War of 1812, Vols. II and VII. The discharge certificate (photographically reproduced in a feature article by E. E. Patton in the Knoxville *Journal*, Aug. 17, 1930, Sec. B, p. 1) of the David Crockett of the *Narrative* reads: "Nashville, March 27, 1815. I certify that David Crockett a 4th Sergt. in my brigade of Tennessee Volunteer Mounted Gun-men, has performed a tour of duty of six months in the service of the United States—that his good conduct, subordination, and valor, under the most trying hardships, entitle him to the gratitude of his country, and that he is hereby HONORABLY discharged by his general. (Signed) John Coffee Brigadier General." No explanation has been found of the discrepancy between 3rd and 4th sergeant as contained in the records quoted.

sure enough they hadn't seen an Indian any more than if they had been all the time chopping wood in my clearing. This closed my career as a warrior, and I am glad of it, for I like life now a heap better than I did then ; and I am glad all over that I lived to see these times, which I should not have done if I had kept fooling along in war, and got used up at it. When I say I am glad, I just mean I am glad I am alive, for there is a confounded heap of things I an't glad of at all. I an't glad, for example, that the "government" moved the deposites, and if my military glory should take such a turn as to make me president after the general's time, I'll move them back ; yes, I, the "government," will "take the responsibility," and move them back again. If I don't, I wish I may be shot.[16]

But I am glad that I am now through war matters,[17] and I reckon the reader is too, for they have no fun in them at all ; and less if he had had to pass through them first, and then to write them afterwards. But for the dullness of their narrative, I must try to make amends by relating some of the curious things that happened to me in private life, and when *forced* to become a public man, as I shall have to be again, if ever I consent to take the presidential chair.

CHAPTER IX.

I CONTINUED at home now, working my farm for two years, as the war finally closed soon after I quit the service. The battle at New Orleans had already been fought, and treaties were made with the Indians which put a stop to their hostilities.

But in this time, I met with the hardest trial which ever falls to the lot of man. Death, that cruel leveller of all distinctions,—to whom the prayers and tears of husbands, and of even helpless infancy, are addressed in vain,—entered my humble cottage, and tore from my children an affectionate good mother, and from me a tender and loving wife.[1]

It is a scene long gone by, and one which it would be supposed I had almost forgotten; yet when I turn my memory back on it, it seems as but the work of yesterday. It was the doing of the Almighty,[2] whose ways are always right, though we sometimes think they fall heavily on us; and

L 2

1. Numerous errors have arisen over the death of Polly Finley Crockett and Crockett's remarriage, the dates of which are unknown. The inscription on the monument to his second wife in Hood County, Tex., states that she married Crockett "in Lawrence County, Tenn., 1815," but this date is impossible because Lawrence County was not created until Oct. 21, 1817. Crockett did not move there until about one month before that date, and Polly did not die until the summer of 1815, after which Crockett's youngest brother, who served in the army three months, lived with him. According to the *Narrative*, a courtship preceded the second marriage, which probably occurred in the spring or summer of 1816 in Franklin County, where Crockett had been elected a lieutenant in the militia on May 21, 1815 (a fact omitted from the *Narrative*). Shackford, *Crockett*, 34; Tennessee State Commission Book, No. 3, Tennessee State Library and Archives, 374.

2. Crockett, by his own admission, was not a religious person. In his letter to George Patton, Jan. 27, 1829 (THS), he says: "I trust that god will give me fortitude [in abstaining from the use of liquor 'Stronger than Cider']. I have never made a pretention to Relegion in my life before. . . ." There is very little of a religious nature in the *Narrative*, yet he may have been essentially and informally religious. He came from and married into families that were religious.

3. John Wesley, William, and Margaret (Polly), in that order. Both Torrence, *Crockett*, 7–8, and French and Armstrong, *Crockett Family*, 341–45, say that Margaret was born in 1812, but it was more likely at the beginning of 1815, as Crockett goes on to say that she was "a mere infant."

4. Crockett's home was Bean's Creek, Franklin County. The widow's name was Elizabeth Patton. She was born in North Carolina, May 22, 1788, and had married a first cousin, James Patton, son of her father's (Robert) brother (Elijah). Her husband had been killed in the Creek War. Shackford, *Crockett*, 34.

5. George and Margaret Ann. Shackford, *Crockett*, 34.

as painful as is even yet the remembrance of her sufferings, and the loss sustained by my little children and myself, yet I have no wish to lift up the voice of complaint. I was left with three children ;[3] the two oldest were sons, the youngest a daughter, and, at that time, a mere infant. It appeared to me, at that moment, that my situation was the worst in the world. I couldn't bear the thought of scattering my children, and so I got my youngest brother, who was also married, and his family to live with me. They took as good care of my children as they well could, but yet it wasn't all like the care of a mother. And though their company was to me in every respect like that of a brother and sister, yet it fell far short of being like that of a wife. So I came to the conclusion it wouldn't do, but that I must have another wife.

There lived in the neighbourhood, a widow lady whose husband had been killed in the war.[4] She had two children, a son and daughter,[5] and both quite small, like my own. I began to think, that as we were both in the same situation, it might be that we could do something for each other ; and I therefore began to hint a little around the matter, as we were once and a while together. She was a good industrious woman, and owned a snug little farm, and lived quite comfortable.[6] I soon began to pay my respects to her in real good earnest; but I was as sly about it as a fox when he is going to rob a hen-roost. I found that my company wasn't at all disagreeable to her; and I thought I could treat her children with so much friendship as to make her a good stepmother to mine, and in this I wan't mistaken, as we soon bargained, and got married, and then went ahead.[7] In a great deal of peace we raised our first crop of children, and they are all married and doing well. But we had a second crop together; and I shall notice them as I go along, as my wife and myself both had a hand in them, and they therefore belong to the history of my second marriage.[8]

The next fall after this marriage, three of my neighbours and myself determined to explore a new country.[9] Their names were Robinson, Frazier, and Rich. We set out for the Creek country, crossing the Tennessee river; and after having made a day's travel, we stop'd at the house of one of my old acquaintances, who had settled there after the war. Resting here a day, Frazier turned out to hunt, being a great hunter; but he got badly bit by a very poisonous snake, and so we left him and went on. We passed through a large rich valley, called Jones's valley,[10] where several

6. Records of both Buncombe County, N. C., and Gibson County, Tenn. (about 1830 most of the family moved to Gibson, not many years after Crockett and Elizabeth went there), show that the Pattons were relatively well-to-do.

7. Crockett's marriage to Elizabeth was performed in the Patton home by Richard Calloway, who later related that Widow Patton's pet pig horned in on the ceremony and was kicked out by Crockett, who announced: "From now on *I'll* be master around here!" Jessie Arn Henderson, "Unmarked Historic Spots of Franklin County," *Tennessee Historical Magazine*, 2nd series, 3 (Jan. 1935), 117–18.

8. Yet this is about the last notice Crockett gives of his "second crop"; it would appear that he was partial to his first set of children, to whom he was writing up to the time of his death. Perhaps there were letters also to the others, but none are extant. The second group of children were Robert Patton (b. 1816), Elizabeth Jane (b. 1818), Rebeckah Elvira (Sissy, b. 1819), and Matilda (b. 1821). Torrence, *Crockett*, 12.

9. This must have been the fall of 1816.

10. In this narrow valley separating the Cahaba River from the Warrior Coal Field is present-day Birmingham. The country was first opened up by the Creek War, when Tennessee troops built a wagon road to Baird's Bluff, near the Blount County (Ala.) line. Many of those Tennesseans sought homes there after the war.

11. On the Black Warrior River. This is the route he had taken going to and from Fort Mims.

12. Crockett, without a doubt, had malaria. It was to trouble him the rest of his life, more than once almost killing him. Among others, see his letters of Feb. 5, 1838 (THS); Feb. 23, 1834 (Boston Public Library); and June 9, 1834 (THS).

other families had settled, and continued our course till we came near to the place where Tuscaloosa now stands.[11] Here we camped, as there were no inhabitants, and hobbled out our horses for the night. About two hours before day, we heard the bells on our horses going back the way we had come, as they had started to leave us. As soon as it was daylight, I started in pursuit of them on foot, and carrying my rifle, which was a very heavy one. I went ahead the whole day, wading creeks and swamps, and climbing mountains; but I couldn't overtake our horses, though I could hear of them at every house they passed. I at last found I couldn't catch up with them, and so I gave up the hunt, and turned back to the last house I had passed, and staid there till morning. From the best calculation we could make, I had walked over fifty miles that day; and the next morning I was so sore, and fatigued, that I felt like I couldn't walk any more. But I was anxious to get back to where I had left my company, and so I started and went on, but mighty slowly, till after the middle of the day. I now began to feel mighty sick, and had a dreadful head-ache.[12] My rifle was so heavy, and I felt so weak, that I lay down by the side of the trace, in a perfect wilderness too, to see if I wouldn't get better.

In a short time some Indians came along. They
had some ripe melons, and wanted me to eat
some, but I was so sick I couldn't. They then
signed to me, that I would die, and be buried ;
a thing I was confoundedly afraid of myself.
But I asked them how near it was to any house ?
By their signs, again, they made me understand it
was a mile and a half. I got up to go ; but when
I rose, I reeled about like a cow with the blind
staggers, or a fellow who had taken too many
" horns."   One of the Indians proposed to go
with me, and carry my gun. I gave him half a
dollar, and accepted his offer. We got to the
house, by which time I was pretty far gone, but
was kindly received, and got on to a bed. The
woman did all she could for me with her warm
teas, but I still continued bad enough, with a high
fever, and generally out of my senses. The next
day two of my neighbours were passing the road,
and heard of my situation, and came to where I
was. They were going nearly the route I had
intended to go, to look at the country ; and so
they took me first on one of their horses, and
then on the other, till they got me back to where
I had left my company. I expected I would get
better, and be able to go on with them, but, instead
of this, I got worse and worse ; and when we got

13. Robinson and Rich (Frazier had been left behind, snake-bitten) and the two newly arrived neighbors who had brought him this far departed.

there, I wan't able to sit up at all. I thought now the jig was mighty nigh up with me, but I determined to keep a stiff upper lip. They carried me to a house, and each of my comrades bought him a horse, and they all set out together, leaving me behind.[18] I knew but little that was going on for about two weeks; but the family treated me with every possible kindness in their power, and I shall always feel thankful to them. The man's name was Jesse Jones. At the end of two weeks I began to mend without the help of a doctor, or of any doctor's means. In this time, however, as they told me, I was speechless for five days, and they had no thought that I would ever speak again,—in Congress or any where else. And so the woman, who had a bottle of Batesman's draps, thought if they killed me, I would only die any how, and so she would try it with me. She gave me the whole bottle, which throwed me into a sweat that continued on me all night; when at last I seemed to make up, and spoke, and asked her for a drink of water. This almost alarmed her, for she was looking every minute for me to die. She gave me the water, and, from that time, I began slowly to mend, and so kept on till I was able at last to walk about a little. I might easily have been mistaken for one of the Kitchen Cabinet, I looked so much like a ghost. I have been particular in giving a history of this sickness, not because I believe it will interest any body much now, nor, indeed, do I *certainly* know that it ever will. But if I should be forced to take the " white house," then it will be good history ; and every one will look on it as important.[14] And I can't, for my life, help laughing now, to think, that when all my folks get around me, wanting good fat offices, how so many of them will say, "What a good thing it was that that kind woman had the bottle of draps, that saved PRESIDENT CROCKETT's life,—the second greatest and best"! ! ! ! ![15] Good, says I, my noble fellow ! You take the post office ; or the navy ; or the war office ; or may-be the treasury. But if I give him the treasury, there's no devil if I don't make him agree first to fetch back them deposites. And if it's even the post-office, I'll make him promise to keep his money 'counts without any figuring, as that throws the whole concern heels over head in debt, in little or no time.[16]

But when I got so I could travel a little, I got a waggoner who was passing along to hawl me to where he lived, which was about twenty miles from my house. I still mended as we went along,

14. Very likely Crockett is making fun of all of the biographies written on Jackson by Reid and Eaton, Waldo, Snelling, and Goodwin. Even Amos Kendall began one but never finished it.

15. Crockett thought the electorate looked on Jackson as the greatest and best, a man who could do no wrong. This "second and best" is meant to be withering sarcasm, aimed at both Jackson and those who regarded Jackson highly.

16. Under one of the postmasters general during Jackson's first administration, William T. Barry of Kentucky (appointed Mar. 9, 1829), huge deficits were discovered in the funds, and Crockett and other Jackson enemies played this for all it was worth in political propaganda. Shackford, *Crockett*, 118–19. See also *Register of Debates*, II, pt. 1, p. 1004; pt. 2, p. 1368; *Congressional Globe*, II, 135, 245; and Crockett letters, *e.g.*, to A. M. Hughes, Feb. 13, 1831.

17. Because most of the Franklin County records are missing, it is impossible to determine precisely when he left. He apparently considered moving to Kentucky at this time, and there is evidence that he spent some time in 1816–17 in the Wolf River section of the present Fentress County, Tenn., then claimed also by Kentucky.

18. Their remaining claims north and east of the Tennessee River, by treaty signed Sept. 20, 1816, by Andrew Jackson, D. Meriwether, and J. Franklin. *American State Papers, Indian Affairs* (Washington, D.C., 1832–34), II, 92–93. Therefore, Crockett moved to Lawrence County after that date.

and when we got to his stopping place, I hired one of his horses, and went on home. I was so pale, and so much reduced, that my face looked like it had been half soled with brown paper.

When I got there, it was to the utter astonishment of my wife; for she supposed I was dead. My neighbours who had started with me had returned and took my horse home, which they had found with their's; and they reported that they had seen men who had helped to bury me; and who saw me draw my last breath. I know'd this was a whapper of a lie, as soon as I heard it. My wife had hired a man, and sent him out to see what had become of my money and other things; but I had missed the man as I went in, and he didn't return until some time after I got home, as he went all the way to where I lay sick, before he heard that I was still in the land of the living and a-kicking.

The place on which I lived was sickly, and I was determined to leave it.[17] I therefore set out the next fall to look at the country which had been purchased of the Chickasaw tribe of Indians.[18] I went on to a place called Shoal Creek, about eighty miles from where I lived, and here again I got sick. I took the ague and fever, which I supposed was brought on me by camping out. I remained here for some time, as I was unable to go farther ; and in that time, I became so well pleased with the country about there, that I resolved to settle in it. It was just only a little distance in the purchase, and no order had been established there ; but I thought I could get along without order as well as any body else. And so I moved and settled myself down on the head of Shoal Creek.[19] We remained here some two or three years, without any law at all ;[20] and so many bad characters began to flock in upon us, that we found it necessary to set up a sort of temporary government of our own. I don't mean that we made any president, and called him the " government," but we met and made what we called a corporation ; and I reckon we called *it* wrong, for it wa'n't a bank, and hadn't any deposites ; and now they call the bank a corporation. But be this as it may, we lived in the back-woods, and didn't profess to know much, and no doubt used many wrong words. But we met, and appointed magistrates and constables to keep order. We didn't fix any laws for them, tho' ; for we supposed they would know law enough, whoever they might be ; and so we left it to themselves to fix the laws.

I was appointed one of the magistrates ;[21] and

M

19. Shoal Creek rises a few miles northeast of the center of Lawrence County (Lawrenceburg) and flows southwest into the Tennessee River at Muscle Shoals. Crockett's holdings are indicated in the Lawrence County Court Minutes, I, recording levies against his land during his financial difficulties, Apr. 4, 1822: "Levied on 160 acres of land lying on the head of Shoal Creek about 3 [incorrectly transcribed by WPA as 30 on p. 502, but given correctly as 3 on p. 503] miles east of Lawrenceburg where Reuben Trip and Thomas Pryer now live supposed to be the property of David Crockett [who had already moved west]." There are three other executions of the same sort issued on the same land.

20. Crockett is in error; it was probably less than a year. He explored the region in the fall of 1816, after the treaty of Sept. 20, and became ill; so it is unlikely that he moved to Shoal Creek before spring 1817. Because the first 11 pages of the minutes are missing, it is unknown exactly when the Lawrence County Court began functioning, but on p. 14, for May 4, 1818, Crockett is listed as a member of the court.

21. Crockett writes as if this was quite some time prior to his being legally and officially appointed. Probably only a few months elapsed after his local appointment before he was named as one of 12 justices of the peace by the state legislature on Nov. 25, 1817, only one month after the creation of the county. *Journal of the House of Representatives*, 1817, pp. 308-12.

22. Brandmarks were usually made in the ears of animals and were registered just as trademarks are today. Court records are filled with the registration of those brandmarks.

23. Lawrence County was not formerly part of Giles County, but of Hickman and Maury counties. Foster, *Counties*, 65–66. It is possible, however, that after the county had been created, but before the county court was established six months later, the unofficial magistrates were in touch with, but not annexed to, neighboring Giles County, which had been created in 1809. Shackford, *Crockett*, 38.

24. The official court record has on the front cover: "David Crockett J. P. Record," but it is the regular journal. (If Crockett kept a private journal, it is not extant.) His resignation, Nov. 1, 1819, is noted, p. 193, and his successor's appointment, p. 198.

when a man owed a debt, and wouldn't pay it, I and my constable ordered our warrant, and then he would take the man, and bring him before me for trial. I would give judgment against him, and then an order of an execution would easily scare the debt out of him. If any one was charged with marking his neighbour's hogs,[22] or with stealing any thing, which happened pretty often in those days,—I would have him taken, and if there was tolerable grounds for the charge, I would have him well whip'd and cleared. We kept this up till our Legislature added us to the white settlements in Giles county;[23] and appointed magistrates by law, to organize matters in the parts where I lived. They appointed nearly every man a magistrate who had belonged to our corporation. I was then, of course, made a squire according to law; though now the honour rested more heavily on me than before. For, at first, whenever I told my constable, says I—"Catch that fellow, and bring him up for trial"—away he went, and the fellow must come, dead or alive; for we considered this a good warrant, though it was only in verbal writings. But after I was appointed by the assembly, they told me, my warrants must be in real writing, and signed; and that I must keep a book, and write my proceedings in it.[24]

This was a hard business on me, for I could just barely write my own name ; but to do this, and write the warrants too, was at least a huckleberry over my persimmon. I had a pretty well informed constable, however ; and he aided me very much in this business. Indeed I had so much confidence in him, that I told him, when we should happen to be out anywhere, and see that a warrant was necessary, and would have a good effect, he need'nt take the trouble to come all the way to me to get one, but he could just fill out one ; and then on the trial I could correct the whole business if he had committed any error. In this way I got on pretty well, till by care and attention I improved my handwriting in such manner as to be able to prepare my warrants, and keep my record book, without much difficulty. My judgments were never appealed from,[25] and if they had been they would have stuck like wax, as I gave my decisions on the principles of common justice and honesty between man and man, and relied on natural born sense, and not on law, learning to guide me ; for I had never read a page in a law book in all my life.

25. Crockett overdoes it; all judgments had to be approved by the court as a whole. The minutes, p. 18 (May 4, 1818), state: "David [transcribed *Daniel* by WPA] Beeler who commenced a suit against John Welch in this court . . . to-gether with John Welch the Defendant . . . mutually agreed to refer said matter . . . [to] David Crockett and William White . . . and . . . do mutually agree to abide by the decision of the said referee who . . . will make report to this court." The conclusion in this case (*ibid.*, 27–28), May 5, 1818, was that John Welch was to pay $5.40 for 108 pounds of pork at $5.00 per 100 pounds and that the parties were to pay "each the one half the cost" accrued in the case. This decision, at least, "stuck like wax." And the trust imposed in Crockett testifies to the truth of his remarks that he tried to give his decrees according to justice. That the court and both parties to a suit agreed to place the decision in Crockett's hands is valuable testimony as to his character. He was poor, but he was, without doubt, honest.

CHAPTER X.

ABOUT the time we were getting under good headway in our new government, a Capt. Matthews came to me and told me he was a candidate for the office of colonel of a regiment, and that I must run for first major in the same regiment.[1] I objected to this, telling him that I thought I had done my share of fighting, and that I wanted nothing to do with military appointments.

He still insisted, until at last I agreed, and of course had every reason to calculate on his support in my election. He was an early settler in that country, and made rather more corn than the rest of us; and knowing it would afford him a good opportunity to electioneer a little, he made a great corn husking, and a great frolic, and gave a general treat, asking every body over the whole country. Myself and my family were, of course, invited. When I got there, I found a very large collection of people, and some friend of mine soon informed me that the captain's son was going to

M 2

1. The jump from lieutenant (held by Crockett in Franklin) to first major would have been a large one, but he actually made colonel. By law each county had at least one regiment, with a colonel and a first and second major. In time of war, there were other gradations in these ranks, including a colonel commandant. Even so, Crockett, when elected, was referred to as lieutenant colonel commandant.

offer against me for the office of major, which he had seemed so anxious for me to get. I cared nothing about the office, but it put my dander up high enough to see, that after he had pressed me so hard to offer, he was countenancing, if not encouraging, a secret plan to beat me. I took the old gentleman out, and asked him about it. He told me it was true his son was going to run as a candidate, and that he hated worse to run against me than any man in the county. I told him his son need give himself no uneasiness about that ; that I shouldn't run against him for major, but against his daddy for colonel. He took me by the hand, and we went into the company. He then made a speech, and informed the people that I was his opponent. I mounted up for a speech too. I told the people the cause of my opposing him, remarking that as I had the whole family to run against any way, I was determined to levy on the head of the mess. When the time for the election came, his son was opposed by another man for major ; and he and his daddy were both badly beaten. [2] I just now began to take a rise, as in a little time I was asked to offer for the Legislature in the counties of Lawrence and Heckman. [3]

I offered my name in the month of February, and started about the first of March with a drove

2. Crockett thus indirectly says that he was elected to the office himself. The entry in the Tennessee State Commission Book, No. 4, p. 96, states: "David Crockett of Laurence [*sic*] county commissioned Lieutenant Colonel Commandant . . . of the 57th Regiment of Militia the 27 March 1818."

3. *Heckman* for *Hickman* perhaps represents Crockett's pronounciation as well as his spelling.

of horses to the lower part of the state of North Carolina.[4] This was in the year 1821, and I was gone upwards of three months. I returned, and set out electioneering, which was a bran-fire new business to me. It now became necessary that I should tell the people something about the government, and an eternal sight of other things that I knowed nothing more about than I did about Latin, and law, and such things as that. I have said before that in those days none of us called Gen'l. Jackson the government, nor did he seem in as fair a way to become so as I do now ; but I knowed so little about it, that if any one had told me he was " the government," I should have believed it, for I had never read even a newspaper in my life, or any thing else, on the subject. But over all my difficulties, it seems to me I was born for luck, though it would be hard for any one to guess what sort. I will, however, explain that hereafter.

I went first into Heckman county to see what I could do among the people as a candidate. Here they told me that they wanted to move their town nearer to the centre of the county, and I must come out in favour of it. There's no devil if I knowed what this meant, or how the town was to be moved ; and so I kept dark, going on the identical same plan that I now find is called " *non-*

4. Crockett's second wife, Elizabeth, was from Swannanoa, Buncombe County, N. C., and her father and at least a sister and a brother still lived there. Swannanoa was on Crockett's route. See Shackford, *Crockett,* 84–86, for a visit of the Crocketts to Swannanoa in the fall of 1827 on their way to Washington, D.C., after Crockett's first election to Congress and for evidence that during the visit he served as a second for Sam Carson in his duel with Dr. Robert Vance.

5. This phrase was being applied to the "Little Red Fox," Vice President Martin Van Buren, by his enemies. What the townspeople meant, of course, was that they wanted the county seat moved to a town nearer the center of the county.

6. On one day, Apr. 1, 1818, as a town commissioner, three years before the date involved here, Crockett signed five depositions "David Crockett" (THS). He is electioneering here in his appeal to the electorate that he is as ignorant and unpretentious and un-"aristocratic" as they are.

7. A gambling expression, of course. It was Crockett's later failure to realize that he could not shuffle and cut with the U. S. bank that destroyed him politically. Shackford, *Crockett*, 161.

committal."[5] About this time there was a great squirrel hunt on Duck river, which was among my people. They were to hunt two days: then to meet and count the scalps, and have a big barbecue, and what might be called a tip-top country frolic. The dinner, and a general treat, was all to be paid for by the party having taken the fewest scalps. I joined one side, taking the place of one of the hunters, and got a gun ready for the hunt. I killed a great many squirrels, and when we counted scalps, my party was victorious.

The company had every thing to eat and drink that could be furnished in so new a country, and much fun and good humour prevailed. But before the regular frolic commenced, I mean the dancing, I was called on to make a speech as a candidate; which was a business I was as ignorant of as an outlandish negro.

A public document I had never seen,[6] nor did I know there were such things; and how to begin I couldn't tell. I made many apologies, and tried to get off, for I know'd I had a man to run against who could speak prime, and I know'd, too, that I wa'n't able to shuffle and cut[7] with him. He was there, and knowing my ignorance as well as I did myself, he also urged me to make a speech. The truth is, he thought my being a candidate was a mere matter of sport; and didn't think, for a moment, that he was in any danger from an ignorant back-woods bear hunter. But I found I couldn't get off, and so I determined just to go ahead, and leave it to chance what I should say. I got up and told the people, I reckoned they know'd what I come for, but if not, I could tell them. I had come for their votes, and if they didn't watch mighty close, I'd get them too. But the worst of all was, that I couldn't tell them any thing about government. I tried to speak about something, and I cared very little what, until I choaked up as bad as if my mouth had been jam'd and cram'd chock full of dry mush. There the people stood, listening all the while, with their eyes, mouths, and years all open, to catch every word I would speak.

At last I told them I was like a fellow I had heard of not long before. He was beating on the head of an empty barrel near the road-side, when a traveler, who was passing along, asked him what he was doing that for? The fellow replied, that there was some cider in that barrel a few days before, and he was trying to see if there was any then, but if there was he couldn't get at it.[8] I told them that there had been a little bit of a speech in me a while ago, but I believed I couldn't get it out.

8. In the margin of a copy in a Nashville library of a largely worthless biography of Crockett—J. S. C. Abbott, *David Crockett: His Life and Adventures* (n.p., New York, 1874)—is a note written by an unknown hand opposite this story: "This speech was made at the present site of Centreville on the north side of the Public Sq." It is so specific as to recommend itself as possibly true.

They all roared out in a mighty laugh, and I told some other anecdotes, equally amusing to them, and believing I had them in a first-rate way, I quit and got down, thanking the people for their attention. But I took care to remark that I was as dry as a powder horn, and that I thought it was time for us all to wet our whistles a little; and so I put off to the liquor stand, and was followed by the greater part of the crowd.

I felt certain this was necessary, for I knowed my competitor could open government matters to them as easy as he pleased. He had, however, mighty few left to hear him, as I continued with the crowd, now and then taking a horn, and telling good humoured stories, till he was done speaking. I found I was good for the votes at the hunt, and when we broke up, I went on to the town of Vernon, which was the same they wanted me to move.[9] Here they pressed me again on the subject, and I found I could get either party by agreeing with them. But I told them I didn't know whether it would be right or not, and so couldn't promise either way.

Their court commenced on the next Monday, as the barbacue was on a Saturday, and the candidates for governor and for Congress, as well as my competitor and myself, all attended.

9. Crockett refers to the disagreement over whether Vernon should remain the county seat. According to the *House Journal*, 1 sess., 1821, p. 300, a bill had been offered "to define the lines of Hickman County & fix the permanent seat of Justice therein"; and in *ibid.*, 2 sess., 1822, are several records (pp. 35, 37, 66)) similar to this one for Tues., July 30, 1822: "Mr. Crockett presented a petition of sundry Citizens of Hickman county, praying that the seat of justice of said county may remain at the town of Vernon." Despite Crockett's petition, the legislature in 1822 moved the county seat to Centerville permanently. Foster, *Counties*, 62–63.

The thought of having to make a speech made my knees feel mighty weak, and set my heart to fluttering almost as bad as my first love scrape with the Quaker's niece. But as good luck would have it, these big candidates spoke nearly all day, and when they quit, the people were worn out with fatigue, which afforded me a good apology for not discussing the government. But I listened mighty close to them, and was learning pretty fast about political matters. When they were all done, I got up and told some laughable story, and quit. I found I was safe in those parts, and so I went home, and didn't go back again till after the election was over. But to cut this matter short, I was elected, doubling my competitor, and nine votes over.[10]

A short time after this, I was in Pulaski, where I met with Colonel Polk, now a member of Congress from Tennessee. He was at that time a member elected to the Legislature,[11] as well as myself ; and in a large company he said to me, " Well, colonel, I suppose we shall have a radical change of the judiciary at the next session of the Legislature." "Very likely, sir," says I, and I put out quicker, for I was afraid some one would ask me what the judiciary was ; and if I knowed I wish I may be shot. I don't indeed believe I had

10. Unfortunately, no records of the votes cast in the elections in which Crockett ran for the legislature have been located.

11. Crockett's memory falters some here. Polk at that time was clerk of the senate. Charles G. Sellers, Jr., *James K. Polk: Jacksonian* (Princeton, 1957), 59. It was during 1823–25, when Crockett was also in the legislature, that Polk was a representative from Maury County. Beginning in 1825, Polk was elected to seven successive terms in Congress; he was thus a fellow representative of Crockett's during all of Crockett's legislative and congressional years. Even before that, however, Crockett had known Polk, whose family had migrated to this section of Tennessee from Mecklenburg County, N. C., which is near Lincoln County, the area David's father left. In 1820, Polk was granted permission to practice law in Lawrence County. Lawrence County Court Minutes, I, 267. In 1821, when Crockett was pretending to have fled from Polk's learning, Polk was a young man of 26, only three years out of the University of North Carolina, and Crockett was 35, a colonel, former justice of the peace, and town commissioner. Therefore, it is not likely that Crockett fled from this youngster in any such fashion. *Ibid., passim.*

12. During this 14th General Assembly, Crockett began his legislative career as a defender of the interests of the "squatters" in West Tennessee by voting for a bill to regulate the surveying of the area. He also voted to call a constitutional convention, but agreed to postpone action to an expected special session. He voted against a bill to "suppress the vice of gaming" and against several divorce applications, including one of former Gov. Joseph McMinn. Shackford, *Crockett*, 50–53; Folmsbee and Catron, "Early Career," 72–73.

13. "Fresh"—freshet. Crockett's statement here explains the entry in the *House Journal*, 1 sess., Sept. 29, 1821, p. 92, only 12 days after the session had commenced: "Ordered, That Mr. Crockett have leave of absence from the service of this house until Thursday next." There is no further record of his presence until Tues., Oct. 9, so he overstayed his leave by four days. Probably the most valuable portion of Edward S. Ellis's *The Life of Colonel David Crockett* (Philadelphia, 1884) is an extract, pp. 58–59, from the "Lawrenceburg (Tenn.) correspondence of the *Cincinnati Gazette* of a recent date," entitled "Davy Crockett's Home: His Old Log House in Tennessee. Mrs. Crockett as a Miller." The extract includes a reminiscence of a "venerable William Simonton" who used to go as a boy to the mill "on the crescent branch of Shoal Creek," where Mrs. Crockett did most of the milling, for Crockett was usually either hunting or electioneering. The house, "a hewed log-building, about 20 x 24," was still standing; the "mill itself is gone, but a portion of the dam can yet be seen when the water is low." Ellis also gives what purports to be an execution judgment issued by Crockett as justice of the peace on Oct. 10, 1818.

ever before heard that there was any such thing in all nature ; but still I was not willing that the people there should know how ignorant I was about it.

When the time for meeting of the Legislature arrived, I went on, and before I had been there long, I could have told what the judiciary was, and what the government was too ; and many other things that I had known nothing about before.[12]

About this time I met with a very severe misfortune, which I may be pardoned for naming, as it made a great change in my circumstances, and kept me back very much in the world. I had built an extensive grist mill, and powder mill, all connected together, and also a large distillery. They had cost me upwards of three thousand dollars, more than I was worth in the world. The first news that I heard after I got to the Legislature, was, that my mills were—not blown up sky high, as you would guess, by my powder establishment,—but swept away all to smash by a large fresh, that came soon after I left home.[13] I had, of course, to stop my distillery, as my grinding was broken up ; and, indeed, I may say, that the misfortune just made a complete mash of me. I had some likely negroes, and a good stock of almost every thing about me, and, best of all, I had an honest wife. She didn't advise me, as is too fashionable, to smuggle up this, and that, and t'other, to go on at home; but she told me, says she, "Just pay up, as long as you have a bit's worth in the world; and then every body will be satisfied, and we will scuffle for more." This was just such talk as I wanted to hear, for a man's wife can hold him devlish uneasy, if she begins to scold, and fret, and perplex him, at a time when he has a full load for a rail-road car on his mind already.

And so, you see, I determined not to break full handed, but thought it better to keep a good conscience with an empty purse, than to get a bad opinion of myself, with a full one.[14] I therefore gave up all I had, and took a bran-fire new start.

N

14. In other words, he decided to pay up his debts and go empty-handed. Chester T. Crowell, "Davy Crockett," *American Mercury* 4 (Jan. 1925), 109, comments: "Whenever he suffered a misfortune he invariably moved." Usually, some debts were left behind, although in this instance Crockett probably left sufficient property to take care of them. As true of other migrating frontiersmen, however, there was more to his successive movements than escape from debt.

CHAPTER XI.

HAVING returned from the Legislature, I determined to make another move, and so I took my eldest son with me, and a young man by the name of Abram Henry, and cut out for the Obion.[1] I selected a spot when I got there, where I determined to settle ; and the nearest house to it was seven miles, the next nearest was fifteen, and so on to twenty.   It was a complete wilderness, and full of Indians who were hunting.[2] Game was plenty of almost every kind, which suited me exactly, as I was always fond of hunting. The house which was nearest me, and which, as I have already stated, was seven miles off, and on the different side of the Obion river, belonged to a man by the name of Owens ; and I started to go there.   I had taken one horse along, to pack our provision, and when I got to the water I hobbled him out to graze, until I got back ; as there was no boat to cross the river in, and it was so

1. The legislature adjourned Sat., Nov. 17 (*House Journal*, 1821, p. 400). Crockett's eldest was John Wesley. The Obion, a tributary of the Forked Deer, which flows into the Mississippi, is a large river in the northwest corner of the state. It has four branches —the North, Middle, and South forks, and the southernmost Rutherford's Fork. Crockett, when he refers to the "Obion" River, usually means its South Fork.

2. The Indian title had been extinguished, however, by the "Jackson Purchase," Oct. 19, 1818, by Andrew Jackson and Isaac Shelby, of all remaining Chickasaw lands west of the northward-flowing Tennessee River. The portion in Tennessee, called the "Western District" and later West Tennessee, was already divided into several counties in 1821. See map in Williams, *West Tennessee*, between pp. 134 and 135.

3. It was now midwinter.

high that it had overflowed all the bottoms and
low country near it.

We now took water like so many beavers, notwithstanding it was mighty cold,[3] and waded on.
The water would sometimes be up to our necks,
and at others not so deep; but I went, of course,
before, and carried a pole, with which I would feel
along before me, to see how deep it was, and to
guard against falling into a slough, as there was
many in our way. When I would come to one,
I would take out my tomahawk and cut a small
tree across it, and then go ahead again. Frequently my little son would have to swim, even
where myself and the young man could wade;
but we worked on till at last we got to the channel
of the river, which made it about half a mile
we had waded from where we took water. I
saw a large tree that had fallen into the river
from the other side, but it didn't reach across.
One stood on the same bank where we were, that
I thought I could fall, so as to reach the other;
and so at it we went with my tomahawk, cutting
away till we got it down; and, as good luck
would have it, it fell right, and made us a way
that we could pass.

When we got over this, it was still a sea of
water as far as our eyes could reach. We took

into it again, and went ahead, for about a mile,
hardly ever seeing a single spot of land, and
sometimes very deep. At last we come in sight
of land, which was a very pleasing thing ; and
when we got out, we went but a little way, before we came in sight of the house, which was
more pleasing than ever ; for we were wet all
over, and mighty cold. I felt mighty sorry when
I would look at my little boy, and see him shak-
ing like he had the worst sort of an ague, for
there was no time for fever then.   As we got
near to the house, we saw Mr. Owens and several men that were with him, just starting away.
They saw us, and stop'd, but looked much astonished until we got up to them, and I made myself known.   The men who were with him
were the owners of a boat which was the first
that ever went that far up the Obion river ;
and some hands he had hired to carry it about
a hundred miles still further up, by water, tho'
it was only about thirty by land, as the river is
very crooked.

They all turned back to the house with me,
where I found Mrs. Owens, a fine, friendly old
woman ; and her kindness to my little boy did
me ten times as much good as any thing she
could have done for me, if she had tried her

best. The old gentleman set out his bottle to us, and I concluded that if a horn wasn't good then, there was no use for its invention. So I swig'd off about a half pint, and the young man was by no means bashful in such a case ; he took a strong pull at it too. I then gave my boy some, and in a little time we felt pretty well. We dried ourselves by the fire, and were asked to go on board of the boat that evening. I agreed to do so, but left my son with the old lady, and myself and my young man went to the boat with Mr. Owens and the others. The boat was loaded with whiskey, flour, sugar, coffee, salt, castings, and other articles suitable for the country ; and they were to receive five hundred dollars to land the load at M'Lemore's Bluff, beside the profit they could make on their load.[4] This was merely to show that boats could get up to that point. We staid all night with them, and had a high night of it, as I took steam enough to drive out all the cold that was in me, and about three times as much more. In the morning we concluded to go on with the boat to where a great *harricane* had crossed the river, and blowed all the timber down into it. When we got there, we found the river was falling fast, and concluded we couldn't get through the timber with-

4. McLemore's Bluff, in Weakley County, on the South Fork, approximately northeast of present Rutherford.

out more rise; so we drop'd down opposite Mr. Owens' again, where they determined to wait for more water.

The next day it rained rip-roriously, and the river rose pretty considerable, but not enough yet. And so I got the boatsmen all to go out with me to where I was going to settle, and we slap'd up a cabin in little or no time. [5] I got from the boat four barrels of meal, and one of salt, and about ten gallons of whiskey.

To pay for these, I agreed to go with the boat up the river to their landing place. I got also a large middling of bacon, and killed a fine deer, and left them for my young man and my little boy, who were to stay at my cabin till I got back; which I expected would be in six or seven days. We cut out, and moved up to the harricane,[6] where we stop'd for the night. In the morning I started about daylight, intending to kill a deer, as I had no thought they would get the boat through the timber that day. I had gone but a little way before I killed a fine buck, and started to go back to the boat; but on the way I came on the tracks of a large gang of elks, and so I took after them. I had followed them only a little distance when I saw them, and directly after I saw two large bucks. I shot one down, and the other wouldn't leave him;

5. Crockett settled in 1822 east of Rutherford's Fork in what was then Carroll County, created in 1821 (Foster, *Counties*, 102), near Rutherford in present Gibson County, which was created, along with Weakley, in 1823. *Ibid.*, 107, 123. The cabin was dismantled in 1934 and brought to Rutherford, where it was rebuilt in 1956. The body of Crockett's mother was later moved from the original grave (at the home of Crockett's brother-in-law) west of Rutherford and reinterred beside the cabin. McBride, "Crockett Memorials," 95.

6. Hurricane thicket, resulting from a hurricane (or an earthquake), is a matted tangle of trees and undergrowth.

7. These tales of Crockett's hunting expeditions cannot be verified. Game was numerous in this wild country. *Life and Adventures* goes into great detail about some of Crockett's hunting expeditions. Stout, "David Crockett," 17, reports that Crockett's former companions contended that he was not the best shot among them, but that he was one of the most successful hunters.

8. A volley of shots or a sudden, effective shot. This is another example of an expression more characteristic of Chilton and of the West in general than of Crockett.

so I loaded my gun, and shot him down too. I hung them up, and went ahead again after my elks. I pursued on till after the middle of the day before I saw them again ; but they took the hint before I got in shooting distance, and run off. I still pushed on till late in the evening, when I found I was about four miles from where I had left the boat, and as hungry as a wolf, for I hadn't eaten a bite that day. [7]

I started down the edge of the river low grounds, giving out the pursuit of my elks, and hadn't gone hardly any distance at all, before I saw two more bucks, very large fellows too. I took a blizzard [8] at one of them, and up he tumbled. The other ran off a few jumps and stop'd ; and stood there till I loaded again, and fired at him. I knock'd his trotters from under him, and then I hung them both up. I pushed on again ; and about sunset I saw three other bucks. I down'd with one of them, and the other two ran off. I hung this one up also, having now killed six that day. I then pushed on till I got to the harricane, and at the lower edge of it, about where I expected the boat was. Here I hollered as hard as I could roar, but could get no answer. I fired off my gun, and the men on the boat fired one too ; but quite contrary to my expectation, they had got through the timber, and were about two miles above me. It was now dark, and I had to crawl through the fallen timber the best way I could; and if the reader don't know it was bad enough, I am sure I do. For the vines and briers had grown all through it, and so thick, that a good fat coon couldn't much more than get along. I got through at last, and went on near to where I had killed my last deer, and once more fired off my gun, which was again answered from the boat, which was still a little above me. I moved on as fast as I could, but soon came to water, and not knowing how deep it was, I halted and hollered till they came to me with a skiff. I now got to the boat, without further difficulty; but the briers had worked on me at such a rate, that I felt like I wanted sewing up, all over. I took a pretty stiff horn, which soon made me feel much better; but I was so tired that I could hardly work my jaws to eat.

In the morning, myself and a young man started and brought in the first buck I had killed; and after breakfast we went and brought in the last one. The boat then started, but we again went and got the two I had killed just as I turned down the river in the evening; and we then pushed on and o'ertook the boat, leaving the other

9. Several critics have pointed to this evidence of a waste of game as symbolic of the philosophy of our nation, which from its earliest beginnings has exploited its natural resources. There is, however, no reason to assume that Crockett never returned to get these particular bucks; in fact, he had hung them up, ostensibly intending to return for them. The woods was near the new home he had just built, and because it was winter the meat would keep for some time.

10. This would be the spring of 1822.

11. Crop.

12. To Shoal Creek, in Lawrence County. By the time of his return several suits had been filed against him, and some judgments had been obtained. For example, Reuben Trip and Thomas Pryer were already occupying his home. Where Crockett's family was living prior to the move to West Tennessee in September is unknown, but they were probably with relatives nearby. Shackford, *Crockett*, 55–56.

two hanging in the woods, as we had now as much as we wanted. [9]

We got up the river very well, but quite slowly; and we landed, on the eleventh day, at the place the load was to be delivered at. They here gave me their skiff, and myself and a young man by the name of Flavius Harris, who had determined to go and live with me, cut out down the river for my cabin, which we reached safely enough.

We turned in and cleared a field, and planted our corn; but it was so late in the spring, we had no time to make rails, and therefore we put no fence around our field.[10] There was no stock, however, nor any thing else to disturb our corn, except the wild *varments*, and the old serpent himself, with a fence to help him, couldn't keep them out. I made corn enough to do me, and during that spring I killed ten bears, and a great abundance of deer. But in all this time, we saw the face of no white person in that country, except Mr. Owens' family, and a very few passengers, who went out there, looking at the country. Indians, though, were still plenty enough. Having laid by my crap,[11] I went home, which was a distance of about a hundred and fifty miles;[12] and when I got there, I was met by an order to attend a call-session of our Legislature.[13] I attended it, and served out my time,[14] and then returned, and took my family and what little plunder I had, and moved to where I had built my cabin, and made my crap.

I gathered my corn, and then set out for my Fall's hunt. This was in the last of October, 1822. I found bear very plenty, and, indeed, all sorts of game and wild varments, except buffalo. There was none of them. I hunted on till Christmass,[15] having supplied my family very well all along with wild meat, at which time my powder gave out; and I had none either to fire Christmass guns, which is very common in that country, or to hunt with. I had a brother-in-law who had now moved out and settled about six miles west of me, on the opposite side of Rutherford's fork of the Obion river, and he had brought me a keg of powder, but I had never gotten it home.[16] There had just been another of Noah's freshes, and the low-grounds were flooded all over with water. I know'd the stream was at least a mile wide which I would have to cross, as the water was from hill to hill, and yet I determined to go on over in some way or other, so as to get my powder. I told this to my wife, and she immediately opposed it with all her might. I still insisted, telling her we had

13. The second session had been called by Gov. William Carroll, Apr. 22, 1822.

14. Crockett also used this phrase to characterize his congressional career under Jackson as service under a "yoke of Bondage." Crockett to Charles Shultz, Dec. 25, 1834 (N.Y. Public Library). With this brief statement Crockett dismisses the called session, during which he introduced a bill "for the relief of Mathias, a free man of color" (and similar bills regarding other persons); unsuccessfully opposed extending the time for filing and adjudicating North Carolina land warrants; and made a speech against fee-grabbing, which was reported in the Nashville press. Shackford, *Crockett*, 57–58; Folmsbee and Catron, "Early Career," 74. The legislature adjourned Aug. 24, 1822.

15. Although this spelling is in the *Narrative*, it is *Chrisemas* the one time it occurs in the letters (to J. L. Totton, Dec. 17, 1827 [Carlos Dew, Trenton, Tenn.]).

16. It is impossible to say which of his numerous brothers-in-law this was. By about 1830 many of them were with him in West Tennessee.

no powder for Christmass, and, worse than all, we were out of meat. She said, we had as well starve as for me to freeze to death or to get drowned, and one or the other was certain if I attempted to go.

But I didn't believe the half of this; and so I took my woolen wrappers, and a pair of mockasins, and put them on, and tied up some dry clothes and a pair of shoes and stockings, and started. But I didn't before know how much any body could suffer and not die. This, and some of my other experiments in water, learned me something about it, and I therefore relate them.

The snow was about four inches deep when I started; and when I got to the water, which was only about a quarter of a mile off, it look'd like an ocean. I put in, and waded on till I come to the channel, where I crossed that on a high log. I then took water again, having my gun and all my hunting tools along, and waded till I came to a deep slough, that was wider than the river itself. I had crossed it often on a log; but, behold, when I got there, no log was to be seen. I knowed of an island in the slough, and a sapling stood on it close to the side of that log, which was now entirely under water. I knowed further, that the water was about eight or ten feet deep under the log, and I judged it to be about three feet deep

over it.   After studying a little what I should do,
I determined to cut a forked sapling, which stood
near me, so as to lodge it against the one that
stood on the island, in which I succeeded very
well.   I then cut me a pole, and crawled along on
my sapling till I got to the one it was lodged
against, which was about six feet above the water.
I then felt about with my pole till I found the log,
which was just about as deep under the water as I
had judged.   I then crawled back and got my
gun, which I had left at the stump of the sapling I
had cut, and again made my way to the place of
lodgement, and then climb'd down the other sapling so as to get on the log.   I then felt my way
along with my feet, in the water, about waist deep,
but it was a mighty ticklish business.   However,
I got over, and by this time I had very little feeling in my feet and legs, as I had been all the time
in the water, except what time I was crossing
the high log over the river, and climbing my lodged
sapling.

I went but a short distance before I came to
another slough, over which there was a log, but
it was floating on the water.   I thought I could
walk it, and so I mounted on it; but when I had
got about the middle of the deep water, somehow or somehow else, it turned over, and in I

O

went up to my head. I waded out of this deep
water, and went ahead till I came to the high-land,
where I stop'd to pull of my wet clothes, and put
on the others, which I had held up with my gun,
above the water, when I fell in.   I got them on,
but my flesh had no feeling in it, I was so cold.
I tied up the wet ones, and hung them up in a bush.
I now thought I would run, so as to warm myself
a little, but I couldn't raise a trot for some time ;
indeed, I couldn't step more than half the length
of my foot.   After a while I got better, and went
on five miles to the house of my brother-in-law,
having not even smelt fire from the time I started.
I got there late in the evening, and he was much
astonished at seeing me at such a time. I staid
all night, and the next morning was most pierc-
ing cold, and so they persuaded me not to go
home that day. I agreed, and turned out and
killed him two deer ; but the weather still got
worse and colder, instead of better.   I staid that
night, and in the morning they still insisted I
couldn't get home. I knowed the water would
be frozen over, but not hard enough to bear me,
and so I agreed to stay that day.   I went out hunting again, and pursued a big *he-bear* all day, but
didn't kill him. The next morning was bitter
cold, but I knowed my family was without meat,

and I determined to get home to them, or die a-trying.

I took my keg of powder, and all my hunting tools, and cut out. When I got to the water, it was a sheet of ice as far as I could see. I put on to it, but hadn't got far before it broke through with me ; and so I took out my tomahawk, and broke my way along before me for a considerable distance. At last I got to where the ice would bear me for a short distance, and I mounted on it, and went ahead ; but it soon broke in again, and I had to wade on till I came to my floating log. I found it so tight this time, that I know'd it couldn't give me another fall, as it was frozen in with the ice. I crossed over it without much difficulty, and worked along till I got to my lodged sapling, and my log under the water. The swiftness of the current prevented the water from freezing over it, and so I had to wade, just as I did when I crossed it before. When I got to my sapling, I left my gun and climbed out with my powder keg first, and then went back and got my gun. By this time I was nearly frozen to death, but I saw all along before me, where the ice had been fresh broke, and I thought it must be a bear straggling about in the water. I, therefore, fresh primed my gun, and, cold as I was, I

17. Crockett could mean Abram Henry, whom he had brought with him from Middle Tennessee, or Flavius Harris, who had accompanied him on his boat trip up the Obion.

was determined to make war on him, if we met. But I followed the trail till it led me home, and I then found it had been made by my young man that lived with me,[17] who had been sent by my distressed wife to see, if he could, what had become of me, for they all believed that I was dead. When I got home I was'nt quite dead, but mighty nigh it ; but I had my powder, and that was what I went for.

CHAPTER XII.

THAT night there fell a heavy rain, and it turned to a sleet. In the morning all hands turned out hunting. My young man, and a brother-in-law[1] who had lately settled close by me, went down the river to hunt for turkeys; but I was for larger game. I told them, I had dreamed the night before of having a hard fight with a big black nigger, and I knowed it was a sign that I was to have a battle with a bear; for in a bear country, I never know'd such a dream to fail. So I started to go up above the harricane, determined to have a bear. I had two pretty good dogs, and an old hound, all of which I took along. I had gone about six miles up the river,[2] and it was then about four miles across to the main Obion; so I determined to strike across to that, as I had found nothing yet to kill. I got on to the river, and turned down it; but the sleet was still getting worse and worse. The bushes were all bent down, and locked together with ice,

o 2

1. This is probably the same brother-in-law mentioned in ch. XI.

2. Rutherford's Fork flows northwest for about 10 miles beyond where Crockett lived and then flows into the Obion at the mouth of the South Fork, which also flows northwest. Crockett seems to have been confused; he must have gone *down* Rutherford's Fork (but in a northerly direction) and then four miles eastward to the South Fork of the Obion.

so that it was almost impossible to get along. In a little time my dogs started a large gang of old turkey goblers, and I killed two of them, of the biggest sort. I shouldered them up, and moved on, until I got through the harricane, when I was so tired that I laid my goblers down to rest, as they were confounded heavy, and I was mighty tired. While I was resting, my old hound went to a log, and smelt it awhile, and then raised his eyes toward the sky, and cried out. Away he went, and my other dogs with him, and I shouldered up my turkeys again, and followed on as hard as I could drive. They were soon out of sight, and ın a very little time I heard them begin to bark. When I got to them, they were barking up a tree, but there was no game there. I concluded it had been a turkey, and that it had flew away.

When they saw me coming, away they went again ; and, after a little time, began to bark as before. When I got near them, I found they were barking up the wrong tree again, as there was no game there. They served me in this way three or four times, until I was so infernal mad, that I determined, if I could get near enough, to shoot the old hound at least. [3] With this intention I pushed on the harder, till I came to the edge of an open parara,[4] and looking on before my dogs, I

3. Some hunters, hunting with bird shot and shotgun, shoot their dogs from a distance so as to sting them for an improper performance, but not to injure them severely. Crockett, however, carries a rifle on this bear hunt, so perhaps in his anger, he means shoot-to-kill.

4. Prairie.

saw in and about the biggest bear that ever was
seen in America. He looked, at the distance he
was from me, like a large black bull. My dogs
were afraid to attack him, and that was the reason
they had stop'd so often, that I might overtake
them. They were now almost up with him, and
I took my goblers from my back and hung them
up in a sapling, and broke like a quarter horse
after my bear, for the sight of him had put new
springs in me. I soon got near to them, but they
were just getting into a roaring thicket, and so I
couldn't run through it, but had to pick my way
along, and had close work even at that.

In a little time I saw the bear climbing up a
large black oak-tree, and I crawled on till I got
within about eighty yards of him. He was setting
with his breast to me ; and so I put fresh priming
in my gun, and fired at him. At this he raised
one of his paws and snorted loudly. I loaded
again as quick as I could, and fired as near the
same place in his breast as possible. At the
crack of my gun here he came tumbling down ;
and the moment he touched the ground, I heard
one of my best dogs cry out. I took my tomahawk in one hand, and my big butcher-knife in
the other, and run up within four or five paces of
him, at which he let my dog go, and fixed his

eyes on me. I got back in all sorts of a hurry, for I know'd if he got hold of me, he would hug me altogether too close for comfort. I went to my gun and hastily loaded her again, and shot him the third time, which killed him good.

I now began to think about getting him home, but I didn't know how far it was. So I left him and started ; and in order to find him again, I would blaze a sapling every little distance, which would show me the way back. I continued this till I got within about a mile of home, for there I know'd very well where I was, and that I could easily find the way back to my blazes. When I got home, I took my brother-in-law, and my young man, and four horses, and went back. We got there just before dark, and struck up a fire, and commenced butchering my bear. It was some time in the night before we finished it ; and I can assert, on my honour, that I believe he would have weighed six hundred pounds. It was the second largest I ever saw. I killed one, a few years after, that weighed six hundred and seventeen pounds. I now felt fully compensated for my sufferings in going after my powder ; and well satisfied that a dog might sometimes be doing a good business, even when he seemed to be *barking up the wrong tree.* We got our meat home, and I had the pleasure to know that we now had plenty, and that of the best ; and I continued through the winter to supply my family abundantly with bear-meat and venison from the woods.

1. This is the present city of Jackson, Tenn.; prior to Aug. 17, 1822, the town was called Alexandria. *Acts of Tennessee*, 1822, pp. 85–86.

2. The doctor was William E. Butler. Of the several anecdotes evolving from Crockett's canvass against Butler, one disclosed that Butler's defeat was caused by Crockett's charging him with aristocratic tendencies—saying that the rugs on Butler's floors were of better material than the wives of the electorate could wear on their backs. J. G. Cisco, "Madison County," *AHM* 8 (Jan. 1903), 29–30. Joseph Lynn and Duncan McIver were members of the Madison County Court; McIver was later in the legislature. Emma Inman Williams, *Historic Madison, the Story of Jackson, and Madison County, Tennessee* (Jackson, 1946), 35n, 527.

CHAPTER XIII.

I HAD on hand a great many skins, and so, in the month of February, I packed a horse with them, and taking my eldest son along with me, cut out for a little town called Jackson,[1] situated about forty miles off. We got there well enough, and I sold my skins, and bought me some coffee, and sugar, powder, lead, and salt. I packed them all up in readiness for a start, which I intended to make early the next morning. Morning came, but I concluded, before I started, I would go and take a horn with some of my old fellow-soldiers that I had met with at Jackson.

I did so ; and while we were engaged in this, I met with three candidates for the Legislature ; a Doctor Butler, who was, by marriage, a nephew to General Jackson, a Major Lynn, and a Mr. McEver, all first-rate men.[2] We all took a horn together, and some person present said to me, " Crockett, you must offer for the Legislature." I told him I lived at least forty miles from any white settlement, and had no thought of becoming a candidate at that time. So we all parted, and I and my little boy went on home.

It was about a week or two after this, that a man came to my house, and told me I was a candidate. I told him not so. But he took out a newspaper [3] from his pocket, and show'd me where I was announced. I said to my wife that this was all a burlesque on me, but I was determined to make it cost the man who had put it there at least the value of the printing, and of the fun he wanted at my expense. So I hired a young man to work in my place on my farm, and turned out myself electioneering. I hadn't been out long, before I found the people began to talk very much about the bear hunter, the man from the cane; [4] and the three gentlemen, who I have already named, soon found it necessary to enter into an agreement to have a sort of caucus at their March court, to determine which of them was the strongest, and the other two was to withdraw and support him. As the court came on, each one of them spread himself, to secure the nomination; but it fell on Dr. Butler, and the rest backed out. The doctor was a clever fellow, and I have often said he was the most talented man I ever

3. The Jackson *Pioneer*, the earliest newspaper in West Tennessee, was first issued in Nov. 1822, two months before the day Crockett refers to here. On May 20, 1824, the Jackson *Gazette* began publication. *Ibid.*, 264.

4. The use of "man from the cane" assumes again that the reader is familiar with *Life and Adventures* in which (pp. 51 ff.) Crockett allegedly acquired the appellation during his first term as a legislator. One of his colleagues, a "Mr. M——l" (almost certainly James C. Mitchell), opposing Crockett on some question, refers to him as "the gentleman from the cane," a reference Crockett and other backwoodsmen then resented. Crockett has his revenge later when he finds the gentleman's cambric ruffle lying in the dust following an altercation; he pins it to his own coarse shirt and walks into the state house of representatives, where the pose is so much appreciated that Mr. M——l retires in embarrassed confusion. The moral victory made Crockett quite popular, and his friends, according to the story, now complimented him as "the gentleman from the cane," in acknowledgment of his having won his spurs.

5. Crockett means that Madison citizens were determined that the representative should come from their county. According to Robert H. White, comp., *Messages of the Governors of Tennessee*, 8 vols. (Nashville, 1952–72), II, 682, Crockett, during the General Assembly of 1823, represented only 10 counties.

6. Col. Adam Alexander was running for Congress at the same time Crockett was a candidate for a seat in the Tennessee General Assembly. (Alexander, of Jackson, was elected for this 1823–25 Congress, and in the succeeding race he defeated Crockett for the seat in 1825–27.)

7. This is a jibe at the "caucus" nomination, for in March the three candidates "elected" Butler to oppose Crockett, the other two dropping out. Crockett is ridiculing this political swapping to win the August election by maneuver.

run against for any office. His being related to Gen'l. Jackson also helped him on very much; but I was in for it, and I was determined to push ahead and go through, or stick. Their meeting was held in Madison county, which was the strongest in the representative district, which was composed of eleven counties, and they seemed bent on having the member from there. [5]

At this time Col. Alexander was a candidate for Congress, and attending one of his public meetings one day, I walked to where he was treating the people, and he gave me an introduction to several of his acquaintances, and informed them that I was out electioneering. [6] In a little time my competitor, Doctor Butler, came along ; he passed by without noticing me, and I suppose, indeed, he did not recognise me. But I hailed him, as I was for all sorts of fun ; and when he turned to me, I said to him, " Well, doctor, I suppose they have weighed you out to me ; but I should like to know why they fixed your election for *March* instead of *August?* [7] This is," said I, " a branfire new way of doing business, if a caucus is to make a representative for the people!" He now discovered who I was, and cried out, " D—n it, Crockett, is that you?"— " Be sure it is," said I, " but I don't want it understood that I have come electioneering. I have just crept out of the cane, to see what discoveries I could make among the white folks." I told him that when I set out electioneering, I would go prepared to put every man on as good footing when I left him as I found him on. I would therefore have me a large buckskin hunting-shirt made, with a couple of pockets holding about a peck each; and that in one I would carry a great big twist of tobacco, and in the other my bottle of liquor; for I knowed when I met a man and offered him a dram, he would throw out his quid of tobacco to take one, and after he had taken his horn, I would out with my twist and give him another chaw. And in this way he would not be worse off than when I found him; and I would be sure to leave him in a first-rate good humour. He said I could beat him electioneering all hollow. I told him I would give him better evidence of that before August, notwithstanding he had many advantages over me, and particularly in the way of money; but I told him that I would go on the products of the country; that I had industrious children, and the best of coon dogs, and they would hunt every night till midnight to support my election; and when the coon fur wa'n't good, I would myself go a wolfing, and shoot down a wolf, and skin his head, and his scalp would be good to me

P

8. The price is accurate, and the brag is not idle. In the Carroll County Court Minutes, 1821–26 (copied by WPA), there are several entries stating that Crockett received bounties for killing wolves. Crockett's rich conversation with Dr. Butler and his leaving of every man in as good a shape as he "found him" are, like so much of the *Narrative*, told almost verbatim in *Life and Adventures*.

9. Another variation of "Stand up to the rack, fodder or no fodder."

10. There was a Milton Brown of Jackson who was congressman for three terms beginning in 1841 (Williams, *Historic Madison*, 529), and he may be the one referred to here. Mr. Shaw has not been identified.

11. Crockett's statement that he did not lose a session is accurate. The Mitchell episode and Crockett's stand in behalf of the Western District while he was still in Middle Tennessee helped him win in his new district.

12. Since the Creek War an enmity had existed between Jackson and Col. John Williams of Knoxville. At the close of the war, Williams was unable to recruit replacements for the heavy casualties of his regiment at Tohopeka, but he refused to obey Jackson's order to turn over to Gen. Nathaniel Taylor's militia some rifles assigned to him by the War Department for use by the regular army troops. Jackson became enraged because he wished Taylor's men, already recruited, to be armed for the Gulf campaigns. See Leota D. Maiden, "Colonel John Williams," ETHS *Publications* 30 (1959), 26–28.

for three dollars, in our state treasury money ;[8] and in this way I would get along on the big string. He stood like he was both amused and astonished, and the whole crowd was in a roar of laughter. From this place I returned home leaving the people in a first-rate way ; and I was sure I would do a good business among them. At any rate, I was determined to stand up to my lick-log, salt or no salt.[9]

In a short time there came out two other candidates, a Mr. Shaw and a Mr. Brown.[10] We all ran the race through; and when the election was over, it turned out that I beat them all by a majority of two hundred and forty-seven votes, and was again returned as a member of the Legislature from a new region of the country, without losing a session.[11] This reminded me of the old saying—" A fool for luck, and a poor man for children."

I now served two years in that body from my new district, which was the years 1823 and '24. At the session of 1823, I had a small trial of my independence, and whether I would forsake principle for party, or for the purpose of following after big men.

The term of Col. John Williams had expired, who was a senator in Congress from the state of Tennessee.[12] He was a candidate for another election,

and was opposed by Pleasant M. Miller, Esq.,
who, it was believed, would not be able to beat
the colonel.[13] Some two or three others were
spoken of, but it was at last concluded that the only
man who could beat him was the present " government," General Jackson. So, a few days before the election was to come on, he was sent for
to come and run for the senate. He was then in
nomination for the presidency;[14] but sure enough
he came, and did run as the opponent of Colonel
Williams, and beat him too, but not by my vote.
The vote was, for Jackson, *thirty-five ;* for Wil
liams, *twenty-five.*[15] I thought the colonel had
honestly discharged his duty, and even the mighty
name of Jackson couldn't make me vote against
him.[16]

But voting against the old chief was found a
mighty up-hill business to all of them except myself. I never would, nor never did, acknowledge
I had voted wrong; and I am more certain now
that I was right than ever.

I told the people it was the best vote I ever
gave; that I had supported the public interest, and
cleared my conscience in giving it, instead of
gratifying the private ambition of a man.

I let the people know as early as then, that I

13. On Apr. 11, 1801, Miller had married Louisa
Blount, daughter of William Blount, governor of the
Southwest Territory and later U.S. senator. Miller
was a member of Congress in 1809–11 and the state
legislature in 1819–22; he migrated to the Western
District in the fall of 1824. Williams, *Historic Madison,* 64–68.

14. By the legislature in 1822.

15. *House Journal,* 1823, pp. 76–77. On Oct. 1,
Crockett offered a motion to delay the vote. Cf. Mar-
quis James, *Andrew Jackson: Portrait of a President*
(New York, 1937), 61, 508n, who says Crockett "led
a successful fight against delay" and cites incorrectly
the Nashville *Whig,* Oct. 6, 1823, which reports
Crockett's motion to delay.

16. Whether Crockett's vote was for the reason
he gives or because of a dislike of Jackson, or both,
is impossible to say.

17. Crockett first used this barb in the letter to A. M. Hughes, Feb. 13, 1831: "Their partizans here reminds me of Some large dogs I have Seen here with their Collers on with letters engraved on the Coller *My dog*—& the Mans Name on the Coller[.]" This seems to be an original observation by Crockett, which cannot be said for most of his political epithets.

18. During these sessions Crockett continued his advocacy of a constitutional convention, but opposed requiring cash payments for Hiwassee District lands, the use of prison labor for internal improvements, and the state banking system. Shackford, *Crockett*, 67–72; Folmsbee and Catron, "Early Career," 76–85. In 1824 he was fined $25 for failing to attend a jury meeting, but it was remitted when he explained that he had been attending the legislature. Gibson County Circuit Court Minutes, Book A (1824–1832), WPA Historical Records Project, 10, 30; Shackford, *Crockett*, 301.

19. The other two candidates were named Ferrell and Persons.

wouldn't take a collar around my neck with the letters engraved on it,

> MY DOG.
>
> ANDREW JACKSON.[17]

During these two sessions of the Legislature, nothing else turned up[18] which I think it worth while to mention ; and, indeed, I am fearful that I am too particular about many small matters ; but if so, my apology is, that I want the world to understand my true history, and how I worked along to rise from a cane-brake to my present station in life.

Col. Alexander was the representative in Congress of the district I lived in, and his vote on the tariff law of 1824 gave a mighty heap of dissatisfaction to his people. They therefore began to talk pretty strong of running me for Congress against him. At last I was called on by a good many to be a candidate. I told the people that I couldn't stand that ; it was a step above my knowledge, and I know'd nothing about Congress matters.

However, I was obliged to agree to run, and myself and two other gentlemen came out.[19] But Pro vidence was a little against two of us this hunt, for it was the year that cotton brought twenty-five dollars a hundred ; and so Colonel Alexander would get up and tell the people, it was all the good effect of this tariff law ; that it had raised the price of their cotton, and that it would raise the price of every thing else they made to sell. I might as well have sung *salms* over a dead horse, as to try to make the people believe otherwise ; for they knowed their cotton had raised, sure enough, and if the colonel hadn't done it, they didn't know what had. So he rather made a mash of me this time, as he beat me exactly *two* votes, as they counted the polls, though I have always believed that many other things had been as fairly done as that same count.[20]

He went on, and served out his term, and at the end of it cotton was down to *six* or *eight* dollars a hundred again ; and I concluded I would try him once more, and see how it would go with cotton at the common price, and so I became a candidate.

P 2

20. Alexander's margin was actually 267; Crockett received 2,599 votes to Alexander's 2,866, according to the returns filed with the secretary of state (the returns of all of Crockett's congressional campaigns are now in Archives Division, Tennessee State Library and Archives; Xerox copies are in Special Collections, Univ. of Tennessee Library, Knoxville). There were other issues, of course, besides the tariff which led to Crockett's defeat. He and a West Tennessee state senator, Col. Thomas Williamson, were attacked during the campaign by John Overton, a close friend of Andrew Jackson, for permitting an East Tennessee brigade to be added to the militia division of the Western District and for legislation changing the times and places of meetings of the courts of Madison County. Jackson *Gazette*, June 18, 1825; Folmsbee and Catron, "Crockett: Congressman," 40–41; Shackford, *Crockett*, 73–74.

1. The years 1825–27. He neglects to mention that on Sept. 24, 1825, he received a land warrant for 20 acres of land in Lawrence County for his War of 1812 service and in October was made foreman of a grand jury. Shackford, *Crockett*, 301; Gibson County Circuit Court Minutes, Book A, 53–54.

2. This is the Obion Lake, located south of Reelfoot Lake, close to the Mississippi and north of present-day Dyersburg.

CHAPTER XIV.

But the reader, I expect, would have no objection to know a little about my employment during the two years while my competitor was in Congress.[1] In this space I had some pretty tuff times, and will relate some few things that happened to me. So here goes, as the boy said when he run by himself.

In the fall of 1825, I concluded I would build two large boats, and load them with pipe staves for market. So I went down to the lake,[2] which was about twenty-five miles from where I lived, and hired some hands to assist me, and went to work; some at boat building, and others to getting staves. I worked on with my hands till the bears got fat, and then I turned out to hunting, to lay in a supply of meat. I soon killed and salted down as many as were necessary for my family; but about this time one of my old neighbours, who had settled down on the lake about twenty-five miles from me, came to my house and told me he wanted me to go down and kill some bears about in his parts. He said they were extremely fat, and very plenty. I know'd that when they were fat, they were easily taken, for a fat bear can't run fast or long. But I asked a bear no favours, no way, further than civility, for I now had *eight* large dogs, and as fierce as painters; so that a bear stood no chance at all to get away from them. So I went home with him, and then went on down towards the Mississippi, and commenced hunting.

We were out two weeks, and in that time killed fifteen bears. Having now supplied my friend with plenty of meat, I engaged occasionally again with my hands in our boat building, and getting staves. But I at length couldn't stand it any longer without another hunt. So I concluded to take my little son, and cross over the lake, and take a hunt there.[3] We got over, and that evening turned out and killed three bears, in little or no time. The next morning we drove up four forks,[4] and made a sort of scaffold, on which we salted up our meat, so as to have it out of the reach of the wolves, for as soon as we would leave our camp, they would take possession. We had just eat our breakfast, when a company of hunters came to our camp, who had fourteen dogs, but all

3. He probably took his youngest son, Robert Patton (of the second marriage), who was nine.

4. No stream or place so named has been located. He might have meant all four forks of the Obion mentioned in note 1, ch. XI.

5. This is Big Clover Lick Creek, which flows into the Obion Lake from the west.

so poor, that when they would bark they would almost have to lean up against a tree and take a rest. I told them their dogs couldn't run in smell of a bear, and they had better stay at my camp, and feed them on the bones I had cut out of my meat. I left them there, and cut out ; but I hadn't gone far, when my dogs took a first-rate start after a very large fat old *he-bear*, which run right plump towards my camp. I pursued on, but my other hunters had heard my dogs coming, and met them, and killed the bear before I got up with him. I gave him to them, and cut out again for a creek called Big Clover, which wa'n't very far off. 5 Just as I got there, and was entering a cane brake, my dogs all broke and went ahead, and, in a little time, they raised a fuss in the cane, and seemed to be going every way. I listened a while, and found my dogs was in two companies, and that both was in a snorting fight. I sent my little son to one, and I broke for t'other. I got to mine first, and found my dogs had a two-year-old bear down, a-wooling away on him; so I just took out my big butcher, and went up and slap'd it into him, and killed him without shooting. There was five of the dogs in my company. In a short time, I heard my little son fire at his bear; when I went to him he had killed it too. He had two dogs in his team. Just at this moment we heard my other dog barking a short distance off, and all the rest immediately broke to him. We pushed on too, and when we got there, we found he had still a larger bear than either of them we had killed, treed by himself. We killed that one also, which made three we had killed in less than half an hour. We turned in and butchered them, and then started to hunt for water, and a good place to camp. But we had no sooner started, than our dogs took a start after another one, and away they went like a thunder-gust, and was out of hearing in a minute. We followed the way they had gone for some time, but at length we gave up the hope of finding them, and turned back. As we were going back, I came to where a poor fellow was grubbing,[6] and he looked like the very picture of hard times. I asked him what he was doing away there in the woods by himself? He said he was grubbing for a man who intended to settle there ; and the reason why he did it was, that he had no meat for his family, and he was working for a little.

I was mighty sorry for the poor fellow, for it was not only a hard, but a very slow way to get meat for a hungry family ; so I told him if he would go with me, I would give him more meat

6. *Grubbing* means to clear the ground of stumps, roots, and stones in preparation for planting crops.

than he could get by grubbing in a month. I intended to supply him with meat, and also to get him to assist my little boy in packing in and salting up my bears. He had never seen a bear killed in his life. I told him I had six killed then, and my dogs were hard after another. He went off to his little cabin, which was a short distance in the brush, and his wife was very anxious he should go with me. So we started and went to where I had left my three bears, and made a camp. We then gathered my meat and salted, and scaffled it, as I had done the other.[7] Night now came on, but no word from my dogs yet. I afterwards found they had treed the bear about five miles off, near to a man's house, and had barked at it the whole enduring night. Poor fellows ! many a time they looked for me, and wondered why I didn't come, for they knowed there was no mistake in me, and I know'd they were as good as ever fluttered. In the morning, as soon as it was light enough to see, the man took his gun and went to them, and shot the bear, and killed it. My dogs, however, wouldn't have any thing to say to this stranger ; so they left him, and came early in the morning back to me.

We got our breakfast, and cut out again ; and we killed four large and very fat bears that day.

7. "Scaffled" is no doubt Crockett's spelling for "scaffolded" (suspended from a scaffold). Crockett's affection for his dogs and his bragging as a hunter are quite typical of the long hunter.

We hunted out the week, and in that time we killed seventeen, all of them first-rate. When we closed our hunt, I gave the man over a thousand weight of fine fat bear-meat, which pleased him mightily, and made him feel as rich as a Jew. I saw him the next fall, and he told me he had plenty of meat to do him the whole year from his week's hunt. My son and me now went home. This was the week between Christmass and New-year that we made this hunt.[8]

When I got home, one of my neighbours was out of meat, and wanted me to go back, and let him go with me, to take another hunt. I couldn't refuse ; but I told him I was afraid the bear had taken to house by that time, for after they get very fat in the fall and early part of the winter, they go into their holes, in large hollow trees, or into hollow logs, or their cane-houses, or the harricanes ; and lie there till spring, like frozen snakes. And one thing about this will seem mighty strange to many people. From about the first of January to about the last of April, these varments lie in their holes altogether. In all that time they have no food to eat ; and yet when they come out, they are not an ounce lighter than when they went to house.[9] I don't know the cause of this, and still I know it is a fact ; and I

8. The last days of 1825.

9. This is simply a good story, contrary to known fact.

leave it for others who have more learning than myself to account for it. They have not a particle of food with them, but they just lie and suck the bottom of their paw all the time. I have killed many of them in their trees, which enables me to speak positively on this subject. However, my neighbour, whose name was McDaniel, and my little son and me, went on down to the lake to my second camp, where I had killed my seventeen bears the week before, and turned out to hunting. But we hunted hard all day without getting a single start. We had carried but little provisions with us, and the next morning was entirely out of meat. I sent my son about three miles off, to the house of an old friend, to get some. The old gentleman was much pleased to hear I was hunting in those parts, for the year before the bears had killed a great many of his hogs. He was that day killing his bacon hogs, and so he gave my son some meat, and sent word to me that I must come in to his house that evening, that he would have plenty of feed for my dogs, and some accommodations for ourselves ; but before my son got back, we had gone out hunting, and in a large cane brake my dogs found a big bear in a cane-house, which he had fixed for his winter-quarters, as they sometimes do.

When my lead dog found him, and raised the yell, all the rest broke to him, but none of them entered his house until we got up. I encouraged my dogs, and they knowed me so well, that I could have made them seize the old serpent himself, with all his horns and heads, and cloven foot and ugliness into the bargain, if he would only have come to light, so that they could have seen him. They bulged in, and in an instant the bear followed them out, and I told my friend to shoot him, as he was mighty wrathy to kill a bear. He did so, and killed him prime. We carried him to our camp, by which time my son had returned; and after we got our dinners we packed up, and cut for the house of my old friend, whose name was Davidson.

We got there, and staid with him that night; and the next morning, having salted up our meat, we left it with him, and started to take a hunt between the Obion lake and the Red-foot lake;[10] as there had been a dreadful harricane, which passed between them, and I was sure there must be a heap of bears in the fallen timber. We had gone about five miles without seeing any sign at all; but at length we got on some high cany ridges, and, as we rode along, I saw a hole in a large black oak, and on examining more closely, I dis-

Q

10. Whether Reelfoot Lake has ever been locally called "Red-foot" is unknown. Perhaps an Indian myth may explain Crockett's spelling. According to this myth (related by Wilbur A. Nelson, "Reelfoot —an Earthquake Lake," *National Geographic* 14 [Jan. 1924], 95–103), Kalopin, meaning *reelfoot* or *clubfoot*, son of a chief of the Chickasaw tribe, stole for his bride the daughter of Copish, chief of the Choctaws, and so brought upon himself and his village the wrath of the Great Spirit, who in his anger stamped his foot upon them and destroyed them. In doing this, Copish left a great footprint which filled with water and came to be called, after the event, Reelfoot Lake. The lake, in Lake and Obion counties in the extreme northwestern tip of Tennessee, was actually created by the earthquakes of 1811–12. For accounts based on authentic source materials, see: the Nelson article, 94–114; "Earthquakes of 1811," *AHM* 5 (1900), 235–37; and Cecil C. Humphreys, "The Formation of Reelfoot Lake and Consequent Land and Social Problems," West Tennessee Historical Society *Papers* 14 (1960), 32–73.

covered that a bear had clomb the tree. I could see his tracks going up, but none coming down, and so I was sure he was in there. A person who is acquainted with bear-hunting, can tell easy enough when the varment is in the hollow; for as they go up they don't slip a bit, but as they come down they make long scratches with their nails.

My friend was a little ahead of me, but I called him back, and told him there was a bear in that tree, and I must have him out. So we lit from our horses, and I found a small tree which I thought I could fall so as to lodge against my bear tree, and we fell to work chopping it with our tomahawks. I intended, when we lodged the tree against the other, to let my little son go up, and look into the hole, for he could climb like a squirrel. We had chop'd on a little time and stop'd to rest, when I heard my dogs barking mighty severe at some distance from us, and I told my friend I knowed they had a bear; for it is the nature of a dog, when he finds you are hunting bears, to hunt for nothing else; he becomes fond of the meat, and considers other game as " not worth a notice," as old Johnson said of the devil.

We concluded to leave our tree a bit, and went to my dogs, and when we got there, sure enough they had an eternal great big fat bear up a tree, just ready for shooting. My friend again petitioned me for liberty to shoot this one also. I had a little rather not, as the bear was so big, but I couldn't refuse ; and so he blazed away, and down came the old fellow like some great log had fell. I now missed one of my dogs, the same that I before spoke of as having treed the bear by himself sometime before, when I had started the three in the cane break. I told my friend that my missing dog had a bear somewhere, just as sure as fate ; so I left them to butcher the one we had just killed, and I went up on a piece of high ground to listen for my dog. I heard him barking with all his might some distance off, and I pushed ahead for him. My other dogs hearing him broke to him, and when I got there, sure enough again he had another bear ready treed ; if he hadn't, I wish I may be shot. I fired on him, and brought him down ; and then went back, and help'd finish butchering the one at which I had left my friend. We then packed both to our tree where we had left my boy. By this time, the little fellow had cut the tree down that we intended to lodge, but it fell the wrong way ; he had then feather'd in on the big tree, to cut that, and had found that it was nothing but a shell on the outside, and all doted [11] in the middle, as too many of

11. "Doted," no doubt derived from *dotage*, means here rotten or decayed with age.

our big men are in these days, having only an outside appearance. My friend and my son cut away on it, and I went off about a hundred yards with my dogs to keep them from running under the tree when it should fall. On looking back at the hole, I saw the bear's head out of it, looking down at them as they were cutting. I hollered to them to look up, and they did so ; and McDaniel catched up his gun, but by this time the bear was out, and coming down the tree. He fired at it, and as soon as it touch'd ground the dogs were all round it, and they had a roll-and-tumble fight to the foot of the hill, where they stop'd him. I ran up, and putting my gun against the bear, fired and killed him. We now had three, and so we made our scaffold and salted them up.[12]

12. Actually they had killed four bears, but one was left, salted, with Davidson.

CHAPTER XV.

In the morning I left my son at the camp, and we started on towards the harricane ; and when we had went about a mile, we started a very large bear, but we got along mighty slow on account of the cracks in the earth occasioned by the earthquakes. We, however, made out to keep in hearing of the dogs for about three miles, and then we come to the harricane. Here we had to quit our horses, as old Nick himself couldn't have got through it without sneaking it along in the form that he put on, to make a fool of our old grandmother Eve. By this time several of my dogs had got tired and come back ; but we went ahead on foot for some little time in the harricane, when we met a bear coming straight to us, and not more than twenty or thirty yards off. I started my tired dogs after him, and McDaniel pursued them, and I went on to where my other dogs were. I had seen the track of the bear they were after, and I knowed he was a screamer. I followed on to about the middle of the harricane ; but my dogs pursued him so close, that they made him climb an old stump about twenty feet high. I got in shooting distance of him and fired, but I was all over in such a flutter from fatigue and running, that I couldn't hold steady ; but, however, I broke his shoulder, and he fell.   I run up and loaded my gun as quick as possible, and shot him again and killed him.   When I went to take out my knife to butcher him, I found I had lost it in coming through the harricane.   The vines and briers was so thick that I would sometimes have to get down and crawl like a varment to get through at all ; and a vine had, as I supposed, caught in the handle and pulled it out.   While I was standing and studying what to do, my friend came to me.   He had followed my trail through the harricane, and had found my knife, which was mighty good news to me ; as a hunter hates the worst in the world to lose a good dog, or any part of his hunting-tools.   I now left McDaniel to butcher the bear, and I went after our horses, and brought them as near as the nature of case would allow.   I then took our bags, and went back to where he was ; and when we had skin'd the bear, we fleeced off the fat and carried it to our horses at several loads.[1] We then packed it up

1. Carried off the bear, of course, not the fleeced-off fat.

on our horses, and had a heavy pack of it on each one. We now started and went on till about sunset, when I concluded we must be near our camp; so I hollered and my son answered me, and we moved on in the direction to the camp. We had gone but a little way when I heard my dogs make a warm start again; and I jumped down from my horse and gave him up to my friend, and told him I would follow them. He went on to the camp, and I went ahead after my dogs with all my might for a considerable distance, till at last night came on. The woods were very rough and hilly, and all covered over with cane.

I now was compel'd to move on more slowly; and was frequently falling over logs, and into the cracks made by the earthquakes, so that I was very much afraid I would break my gun. However I went on about three miles, when I came to a good big creek, which I waded.[2] It was very cold, and the creek was about knee-deep; but I felt no great inconvenience from it just then, as I was all over wet with sweat from running, and I felt hot enough. After I got over this creek and out of the cane, which was very thick on all our creeks, I listened for my dogs. I found they had either treed or brought the bear to a stop, as they

2. This creek could be any one of several. Crockett, his son, and McDaniel are hunting between Obion and Reelfoot lakes and might have reached the upper limits of Reelfoot River.

continued barking in the same place. I pushed on as near in the direction to the noise as I could, till I found the hill was too steep for me to climb, and so I backed and went down the creek some distance till I came to a hollow, and then took up that, till I come to a place where I could climb up the hill. It was mighty dark, and was difficult to see my way or any thing else. When I got up the hill, I found I had passed the dogs; and so I turned and went to them. I found, when I got there, they had treed the bear in a large forked poplar, and it was setting in the fork.

I could see the lump, but not plain enough to shoot with any certainty, as there was no moonlight; and so I set in to hunting for some dry brush to make me a light; but I could find none, though I could find that the ground was torn mightily to pieces by the cracks.

At last I thought I could shoot by guess, and kill him; so I pointed as near the lump as I could, and fired away. But the bear didn't come he only clomb up higher, and got out on a limb, which helped me to see him better. I now loaded up again and fired, but this time he didn't move at all. I commenced loading for a third fire, but the first thing I knowed, the bear was down among my dogs, and they were fighting all around me.

I had my big butcher in my belt, and I had a pair of dressed buckskin breeches on. So I took out my knife, and stood, determined, if he should get hold of me, to defend myself in the best way I could. I stood there for some time, and could now and then see a white dog I had, but the rest of them, and the bear, which were dark coloured, I couldn't see at all, it was so miserable dark. They still fought around me, and sometimes within three feet of me ; but, at last, the bear got down into one of the cracks, that the earthquakes had made in the ground, about four feet deep, and I could tell the biting end of him by the hollering of my dogs. So I took my gun and pushed the muzzle of it about, till I thought I had it against the main part of his body, and fired ; but it happened to be only the fleshy part of his foreleg. With this, he jumped out of the crack, and he and the dogs had another hard fight around me, as before. At last, however, they forced him back into the crack again, as he was when I had shot.

I had laid down my gun in the dark, and I now began to hunt for it ; and, while hunting, I got hold of a pole, and I concluded I would punch him awhile with that. I did so, and when I would punch him, the dogs would jump in on

3. Stout, "Crockett," 19, states that this story of Crockett's killing a bear in one of the "cracks," or fissures, at night was told to him by a "reliable person in Gibson County" in 1843–44. Stout adds that it is "a parallel of the story of General Putnam and the wolf, I believe never before in print." The story of Gen. Putnam's "victory over the she-wolf" is told in Oliver W. B. Peabody, *Life of Israel Putnam*, American Biography Series, ed. Jared Sparks, VIII (New York, 1902), 7.

4. It is early Jan. 1826.

him, when he would bite them badly, and they would jump out again. I concluded, as he would take punching so patiently, it might be that he would lie still enough for me to get down in the crack, and feel slowly along till I could find the right place to give him a dig with my butcher. So I got down, and my dogs got in before him and kept his head towards them, till I got along easily up to him; and placing my hand on his rump, felt for his shoulder, just behind which I intended to stick him. I made a lounge with my long knife, and fortunately stuck him right through the heart; at which he just sank down, and I crawled out in a hurry. In a little time my dogs all come out too, and seemed satisfied, which was the way they always had of telling me that they had finished him.[3]

I suffered very much that night with cold, as my leather breeches, and every thing else I had on, was wet and frozen. But I managed to get my bear out of this crack after several hard trials, and so I butchered him, and laid down to try to sleep. But my fire was very bad, and I couldn't find any thing that would burn well to make it any better; and I concluded I should freeze, if I didn't warm myself in some way by exercise.[4] So I got up, and hollered a while, and then I would just jump up and down with all my might, and throw myself into all sorts of motions. But all this wouldn't do; for my blood was now getting cold, and the chills coming all over me. I was so tired, too, that I could hardly walk; but I thought I would do the best I could to save my life, and then, if I died, nobody would be to blame. So I went to a tree about two feet through, and not a limb on it for thirty feet, and I would climb up it to the limbs, and then lock my arms together around it, and slide down to the bottom again. This would make the insides of my legs and arms feel mighty warm and good. I continued this till daylight in the morning, and how often I clomb up my tree and slid down I don't know, but I reckon at least a hundred times.

In the morning I got my bear hung up so as to be safe, and then set out to hunt for my camp. I found it after a while, and McDaniel and my son were very much rejoiced to see me get back, for they were about to give me up for lost. We got our breakfasts, and then secured our meat by building a high scaffold, and covering it over. We had no fear of its spoiling, for the weather was so cold that it couldn't.

We now started after my other bear, which had caused me so much trouble and suffering; and before we got him, we got a start after another, and took him also. We went on to the creek I had crossed the night before and camped, and then went to where my bear was, that I had killed in the crack. When we examined the place, McDaniel said he wouldn't have gone into it, as I did, for all the bears in the woods.

We took the meat down to our camp and salted it, and also the last one we had killed; intending, in the morning, to make a hunt in the harricane again.

We prepared for resting that night, and I can assure the reader I was in need of it. We had laid down by our fire, and about ten o'clock there came a most terrible earthquake, which shook the earth so, that we were rocked about like we had been in a cradle. We were very much alarmed; for though we were accustomed to feel earthquakes, we were now right in the region which had been torn to pieces by them in 1812, and we thought it might take a notion and swallow us up, like the big fish did Jonah.

In the morning we packed up and moved to the harricane, where we made another camp, and turned out that evening and killed a very large bear, which made *eight* we had now killed in this hunt.

The next morning we entered the harricane again, and in little or no time my dogs were in full cry. We pursued them, and soon came to a thick cane-brake, in which they had stop'd their bear. We got up close to him, as the cane was so thick that we couldn't see more than a few feet. Here I made my friend hold the cane a little open with his gun till I shot the bear, which was a mighty large one. I killed him dead in his tracks. We got him out and butchered him, and in a little time started another and killed him, which now made *ten* we had killed; and we know'd we couldn't pack any more home, as we had only five horses along; therefore we returned to the camp and salted up all our meat, to be ready for a start homeward next morning.[5]

The morning came, and we packed our horses with the meat, and had as much as they could possibly carry, and sure enough cut out for home. It was about thirty miles, and we reached home the second day. I had now accommodated my neighbour with meat enough to do him, and had killed in all, up to that time, fifty-eight bears, during the fall and winter.

As soon as the time come for them to quit their houses and come out again in the spring,

R

5. Some writers have pointed to a previous instance as being one of profligacy in the killing of game, but here certainly it is not the case—the hunters could carry no more meat home, so they stopped killing bears.

6. This number would be outstanding for one hunter in only a fall, winter, and spring. Although he does not say so, he may be including the bears killed by those who went with him. The natural conditions surrounding Reelfoot Lake and the fact that this territory had just recently been opened, however, make Crockett's story entirely possible. Stout, "Crockett," 17 ff., in recounting some reminiscences given him in 1843–44 by Crockett's old associates, quotes a former sheriff of Gibson County, Mr. McLaurin, as claiming to have beaten Crockett in a shooting contest once for a $500 prize, while freely admitting that Crockett surpassed him as a hunter. There are other reliable sources to establish that Crockett was a successful bear hunter. See H. S. Turner, "Andrew Jackson and David Crockett: Reminiscences, " *Magazine of American History* 27 (May 1892), 385–87, for recollections of Col. Robert Chester, who had slept on bear rugs in Crockett's house. (Col. Chester's first wife was a niece of Andrew Jackson.)

I took a notion to hunt a little more, and in about one month I killed forty-seven more, which made one hundred and five bears I had killed in less than one year from that time.[6]

CHAPTER XVI.

HAVING now closed my hunting for that winter, I returned to my hands, who were engaged about my boats and staves, and made ready for a trip down the river.[1] I had two boats and about thirty thousand staves, and so I loaded with them, and set out for New Orleans. I got out of the Obion river, in which I had loaded my boats, very well; but when I got into the Mississippi, I found all my hands were bad scared,[2] and in fact I believe I was scared a little the worst of any; for I had never been down the river, and I soon discovered that my pilot was as ignorant of the business as myself. I hadn't gone far before I determined to lash the two boats together; we did so, but it made them so heavy and obstinate, that it was next akin to impossible to do any thing at all with them, or to guide them right in the river.

That evening we fell in company with some Ohio boats; and about night we tried to land, but we could not. The Ohio men hollered to us to

1. The late winter and spring of 1826.

2. Scarred. Crockett seems to be punning on the pronounciation of both "scarred" and "scared." This sounds more like Chilton than Crockett, however.

go on and run all night. We took their advice, though we had a good deal rather not ; but we couldn't do any other way. In a short distance we got into what is called the " *Devil's Elbow;*" and if any place in the wide creation has its own proper name, I thought it was this. Here we had about the hardest work that I ever was engaged in, in my life, to keep out of danger ; and even then we were in it all the while. We twice attempted to land at Wood-yards, which we could see, but couldn't reach.

The people would run out with lights, and try to instruct us how to get to shore ; but all in vain. Our boats were so heavy that we couldn't take them much any way, except the way they wanted to go, and just the way the current would carry them. At last we quit trying to land, and concluded just to go ahead as well as we could, for we found we couldn't do any better. Some time in the night I was down in the cabin of one of the boats, sitting by the fire, thinking on what a hobble we had got into ; and how much better bear-hunting was on hard land, than floating along on the water, when a fellow had to go ahead whether he was exactly willing or not.

The hatchway into the cabin came slap down, right through the top of the boat ; and it was the only way out except a small hole in the side, which we had used for putting our arms through to dip up water before we lashed the boats together.

We were now floating sideways, and the boat I was in was the hindmost as we went. All at once I heard the hands begin to run over the top of the boat in great confusion, and pull with all their might; and the first thing I know'd after this we went broadside full tilt against the head of an island where a large raft of drift timber had lodged. The nature of such a place would be, as every body knows, to suck the boats down, and turn them right under this raft; and the uppermost boat would, of course, be suck'd down and go under first. As soon as we struck, I bulged for my hatchway, as the boat was turning under sure enough. But when I got to it, the water was pouring thro' in a current as large as the hole would let it, and as strong as the weight of the river could force it. I found I couldn't get out here, for the boat was now turned down in such a way, that it was steeper than a house-top. I now thought of the hole in the side, and made my way in a hurry for that. With difficulty I got to it, and when I got there, I found it was too small for me to get out by my own dower,[3] and I began

R 2

3. Meaning by his own strength.

to think that I was in a worse box than ever.
But I put my arms through and hollered as loud
as I could roar, as the boat I was in hadn't yet
quite filled with water up to my head, and the
hands who were next to the raft, seeing my arms
out, and hearing me holler, seized them, and began to pull. I told them I was sinking, and to
pull my arms off, or force me through, for now I
know'd well enough it was neck or nothing, come
out or sink.

By a violent effort they jerked me through ;
but I was in a pretty pickle when I got through.
I had been sitting without any clothing over my
shirt : this was torn off, and I was literally
skin'd like a rabbit.[4] I was, however, well pleased
to get out in any way, even without shirt or
hide ; as before I could straighten myself on the
boat next to the raft, the one they pull'd me out
of went entirely under, and I have never seen it
any more to this day. We all escaped on to the
raft, where we were compelled to sit all night,
about a mile from land on either side. Four of
my company were bareheaded, and three bare-
footed ; and of that number I was one. I reckon
I looked like a pretty cracklin ever to get to
Congress ! ! !

We had now lost all our loading ; and every

4. Accounts, supposedly historical, of this event
are in Davis, *History of Memphis*, 146–50, and J. M.
Keating, *History of the City of Memphis and Shelby
County Tennessee*, 3 vols. (Syracuse, 1888), I, 180–
81. Both state that in the disaster, within sight of
Memphis just above "Paddy's Hen-and-Chickens,"
the boat was torn in two by a "sawyer" (a sunken
tree, gyrating in and parallel to the flow of the current) and that when the townspeople from Memphis
arrived by boat, Crockett was sitting in a completely
nude state.

particle of our clothing, except what little we had on ; but over all this, while I was setting there, in the night, floating about on the drift, I felt happier and better off than I ever had in my life before, for I had just made such a marvellous escape, that I had forgot almost every thing else in that ; and so I felt prime.

In the morning about sunrise, we saw a boat coming down, and we hailed her. They sent a large skiff, and took us all on board, and carried us down as far as Memphis. Here I met with a friend, that I never can forget as long as I am able to go ahead at any thing ; it was a Major Winchester,[5] a merchant of that place : he let us all have hats, and shoes, and some little money to go upon, and so we all parted.

A young man and myself concluded to go on down to Natchez, to see if we could hear any thing of our boats ; for we supposed they would float out from the raft, and keep on down the river. We got on a boat at Memphis, that was going down, and so cut out. Our largest boat, we were informed, had been seen about fifty miles below where we stove, and an attempt had been made to land her, but without success, as she was as hardheaded as ever.

This was the last of my boats, and of my boat-

5. Marcus B. Winchester, postmaster of Memphis. According to Davis, *History of Memphis*, 150, Crockett, reattired and warmed by a "horn" or two, told stories and anecdotes, so pleasing Winchester that he urged Crockett to become a candidate for Congress. "It may be," Winchester said, "that the misfortune at the head of the Old Hen was the starting point of his future importance and notoriety." There is no doubt that Winchester was one of Crockett's strong supporters, even as late as July 3, 1831, when Judge John Overton wrote Winchester, calling him and the people of Memphis to task for their continued support of Crockett after he became anti-Jackson. Keating, *Memphis*, I, 178–79.

6. Crockett has omitted any mention of a year in his life, for the hunting episodes ended in spring 1826. His trip to Natchez (which may have involved a good part of the year) was in spring 1827; the congressional elections were in Aug. 1827. That Crockett had much bad luck is undeniable; financially, he could ill afford the loss of his boats. For electioneering he required money to buy liquor (although it was cheap in those days), and he got some from a friend, who may well have been Winchester. Shackford, *Crockett,* 79.

ing ; for it went so badly with me, along at the first, that I hadn't much mind to try it any more. I now returned home again, and as the next August was the Congressional election, I began to turn my attention a little to that matter, as it was beginning to be talked of a good deal among the people.[6]

CHAPTER XVII.

I HAVE, heretofore, informed the reader that I had determined to run this race to see what effect *the price of cotton* could have again on it. I now had Col. Alexander to run against once more, and also General William Arnold.[1]

I had difficulties enough to fight against this time, as every one will suppose; for I had no money, and a very bad prospect, so far as I know'd, of getting any to help me along. I had, however, a good friend, who sent for me to come and see him.[2] I went, and he was good enough to offer me some money to help me out. I borrowed as much as I thought I needed at the start, and went ahead. My friend also had a good deal of business about over the district at the different courts; and if he now and then slip'd in a good word for me, it is nobody's business. We frequently met at different places, and, as he thought I needed, he would occasionally hand me a little more cash; so I was able to buy

1. Gen. (then Col.) William Arnold, appointed as one of the three commissioners for the city of Jackson by legislative act on Aug. 17, 1822, had defeated the noted Col. Robert H. Dyer in 1824 for major general of the old Third Division. Williams, *Historic Madison*, 37–38, 54. Crockett's opponents, then, were rather formidable men. Although his campaigning is often dismissed as a clowning act which amused the crowds and thereby procured votes, this is not all of the truth.

2. Probably Marcus B. Winchester, who as a merchant-postmaster might have, as mentioned below, "a good deal of business about over the district at the different courts."

3. The actual returns (1827) : Crockett, 5,868;
Alexander, 3,646; and Arnold, 2,417; giving Crockett a plurality of 2,223 votes.

a little of " the *creature*," to put my friends in a
good humour, as well as the other gentlemen, for
they all treat in that country ; not to get elected,
of course—for that would be against the law ; but
just, as I before said, to make themselves and their
friends feel their keeping a little.

Nobody ever did know how I got money to
get along on, till after the election was over, and
I had beat my competitors twenty-seven hundred and forty-eight votes.[3] Even the price of
cotton couldn't save my friend Aleck this time.
My rich friend, who had been so good to me in
the way of money, now sent for me, and loaned
me a hundred dollars, and told me to go ahead ;
that that amount would bear my expenses to Congress, and I must then shift for myself. I came
on to Washington, and draw'd two hundred and
fifty dollars, and purchased with it a check on the
bank at Nashville, and enclosed it to my friend ;
and I may say, in truth, I sent this money with a
mighty good will, for I reckon nobody in this
world loves a friend better than me, or remembers
a kindness longer.

I have now given the close of the election, but
I have skip'd entirely over the canvass, of which
I will say a very few things in this place ; as I
know very well how to tell the truth, but not much

about placing them in book order, so as to please critics.

Col. Alexander was a very clever fellow, and principal surveyor at that time ; so much for one of the men I had to run against.   My other competitor was a major-general in the militia, and an attorney-general at the law, and quite a smart, clever man also ; and so it will be seen I had war work as well as law trick, to stand up under.   Taking both together, they make a pretty considerable of a load for any one man to carry.   But for war claims, I consider myself behind no man except "the government," and mighty little, if any, behind him ; but this the people will have to determine hereafter, as I reckon it won't do to quit the work of "reform and retrenchment" yet for a spell.

But my two competitors seemed some little afraid of the influence of each other, but not to think me in their way at all.   They, therefore, were generally working against each other, while I was going ahead for myself, and mixing among the people in the best way I could.   I was as cunning as a little red fox, and wouldn't risk my tail in a "committal" trap.[4]

I found the sign was good, almost everywhere I went.   On one occasion, while we were in the

4. Without identifying himself with Martin Van Buren, whom Crockett disliked intensely, he nevertheless employs here with reference to himself a term he often used against Van Buren—that he was as slick and cunning as a little red fox and that his prime characteristic was one of shrewd noncommitment.

eastern counties of the district, it happened that we all had to make a speech, and it fell on me to make the first one. I did so after my manner, and it turned pretty much on the old saying, " A short horse is soon curried," as I spoke not very long. Colonel Alexander followed me, and then General Arnold come on.

The general took much pains to reply to Alexander, but didn't so much as let on that there was any such candidate as myself at all. He had been speaking for a considerable time, when a large flock of guinea-fowls came very near to where he was, and set up the most unmerciful chattering that ever was heard, for they are a noisy little brute any way. They so confused the general, that he made a stop, and requested that they might be driven away. I let him finish his speech, and then walking up to him, said aloud, " Well, colonel, you are the first man I ever saw that understood the language of fowls." I told him that he had not had the politeness to name me in his speech, and that when my little friends, the guinea-fowls, had come up and began to holler " Crockett, Crockett, Crockett," he had been ungenerous enough to stop, and drive *them* all away. This raised a universal shout among the people for me, and the general seemed mighty bad plagued. But he got more plagued than this at the polls in August, as I have stated before.

This election was in 1827, and I can say, on my conscience, that I was, without disguise, the friend and supporter of General Jackson, upon his principles as he laid them down, and as "*I understood them*," before his election as president.[5] During my two first sessions in Congress, Mr. Adams[6] was president, and I worked along with what was called the Jackson party pretty well. I was re-elected to Congress, in 1829, by an overwhelming majority ;[7] and soon after the commencement of this second term, I saw, or thought I did, that it was expected of me that I was to bow to the name of Andrew Jackson, and follow him in all his motions, and mindings, and turnings, even at the expense of my conscience and judgment. Such a thing was new to me, and a total stranger to my principles. I know'd well enough, though, that if I didn't " hurra" for his name, the hue and cry was to be raised against me, and I was to be sacrificed, if possible.[8] His famous, or rather I should say his in-*famous*, Indian bill was brought forward, and I opposed it from the purest motives in the world.[9] Several of my colleagues got around me, and told me how well they loved me, and that I was ruining my-

S

5. That Crockett was a friend and supporter of Jackson at this point is quite true. Crockett's personal letters show that at least through Mar. 11, 1828, he was still talking pro-Jackson, but something happened between sessions of his first term. The clue to this is in a letter (Dec. 13, 1828) he wrote to the Jackson *Gazette* (printed in the Jan. 3, 1829, issue) announcing his intention to introduce an amendment to Polk's Tennessee land bill that would more adequately protect the interests of West Tennessee "squatters." It was the refusal of his Jacksonian colleagues to shift their support from Polk's bill to his and their unsuccessful efforts to defeat him for re-election in Aug. 1829 which led to his break with Jackson.

6. John Quincy Adams.

7. The actual returns (1829) gave Alexander 3,641 votes; Estes, 156; Clark, 12; and Crockett, 6,773, a plurality of 3,132.

8. There is no question that President Jackson demanded full allegiance and tended to interpret any difference of opinion as a difference of allegiance.

9. Crockett cast the only Tennessee vote against it.

10. Crockett first used this expression in a letter to
Dr. Calvin Jones, Aug. 22, 1831 (Ed K. Boyd, Boli-
var, Tenn.) : "I would rather be politically buried
than to be hypochritically imortalized." The letter
also contains a variant of the "My Dog" phrase: "I
would rather be beaten and be a man than to be
elected and be a little puppy dog."

self. They said this was a favourite measure of
the president, and I ought to go for it. I told
them I believed it was a wicked, unjust measure,
and that I should go against it, let the cost to myself be what it might ; that I was willing to go
with General Jackson in every thing that I believed was honest and right ; but, further than
this, I wouldn't go for him, or any other man in
the whole creation ; that I would sooner be honestly and politically d—nd, than hypocritically
immortalized.[10] I had been elected by a majority
of three thousand five hundred and eighty-five
votes, and I believed they were honest men, and
wouldn't want me to vote for any unjust notion,
to please Jackson or any one else ; at any rate,
I was of age, and was determined to trust them.
I voted against this Indian bill, and my conscience
yet tells me that I gave a good honest vote, and
one that I believe will not make me ashamed in
the day of judgment.   I served out my term, and
though many amusing things happened, I am not
disposed to swell my narrative by inserting them.

When it closed, and I returned home, I found
the storm had raised against me sure enough ;
and it was echoed from side to side, and from end
to end of my district, that I had turned against
Jackson. This was considered the unpardonable

sin. I was hunted down like a wild varment, and in this hunt every little newspaper in the district, and every little pin-hook lawyer was engaged. Indeed, they were ready to print any and every thing that the ingenuity of man could invent against me. Each editor was furnished with the journals of Congress from head-quarters; and hunted out every vote I had missed in four sessions, whether from sickness[11] or not, no matter; and each one was charged against me at *eight* dollars. In all I had missed about *seventy* votes, which they made amount to five hundred and sixty dollars; and they contended I had swindled the government out of this sum, as I had received my pay, as other members do. I was now again a candidate in 1830,[12] while all the attempts were making against me; and every one of these little papers kept up a constant war on me, fighting with every scurrilous report they could catch.[13]

Over all I should have been elected, if it hadn't been, that but a few weeks before the election, the little four-pence-ha'penny limbs of the law fell on a plan to defeat me, which had the desired effect. They agreed to spread out over the district, and make appointments for me to speak, almost everywhere, to clear up the Jackson question. They would give me no notice of these appointments,

11. For evidence of Crockett's illness during his first term, see his letter to James Blackburn, Feb. 5, 1828. For later sicknesses, see letters of Feb. 23 and June 9, 1834 (THS).

12. The election was in Aug. 1831, but the canvass always started early. The Jackson *Gazette*, in Crockett's district, not only printed the alleged remarks by Crockett against the Indian removal bill, along with an editorial denouncing his vote, but also claimed in August that Crockett had deserted the Jackson ranks and suggested that Congressman Thomas Chilton of Kentucky was partly responsible.

13. Crockett had other problems too. In 1828 and 1829 he was listed in the First Minute Book of the County Court of Weakley County, I, 24, 89, as delinquent in the payment of taxes on 200 acres of land. In May 1831 he sold some of the land to his brother-in-law, George Patton, for $100 and in December sold him for $300 "one Negro girl named Adeline." Deed Records and bill of sale transcribed in French and Armstrong, *Crockett Family*, 378, 546. There are Crockett letters from Weakley County dated Aug. 22, 1831; Jan. 7, 1832 (Historical Society of Pennsylvania); Aug. 11 and Oct. 31, 1835 (Mrs. Isabel V. Powell, Portland, Maine), the second also saying "at home." Yet, on May 26, 1834 (J. E. Wallis, Los Angeles), he wrote: "My Post Office is called Crocketts P. O.—in Gibson County." As a congressman, Crockett gave his residence in 1827 as Trenton and in 1829 and 1833 as Crockett (a post office in Gibson County was established with this name Dec. 12, 1829; renamed China Grove Apr. 1, 1836; and discontinued Nov. 13, 1846). Record Group 28, National Archives. Apparently, Crockett had two homes, one in Gibson and the other in Weakley.

and the people would meet in great crowds to hear what excuse Crockett had to make for quitting Jackson.

But instead of Crockett's being there, this small-fry of lawyers would be there, with their saddle-bags full of the little newspapers and their journals of Congress; and would get up and speak, and read their scurrilous attacks on me, and would then tell the people that I was afraid to attend; and in this way would turn many against me. All this intrigue was kept a profound secret from me, till it was too late to counteract it; and when the election came, I had a majority in seventeen counties, putting all their votes together, but the eighteenth beat me; and so I was left out of Congress during those two years.[14] The people of my district were induced, by these tricks, to take a stay on me for that time; but they have since found out that they were imposed on, and on re-considering my case, have reversed that decision; which, as the Dutchman said, "is as fair a ding as eber was."

When I last declared myself a candidate, I knew that the district would be divided by the Legislature before the election would come on; and I moreover knew, that from the geographical situation of the country, the county of Madison,

14. According to official returns Crockett received 7,948 votes and William Fitzgerald, a lawyer of Dresden, Tenn., 8,534. The 18th county, Madison (home of the Jackson *Gazette*), was carried by Fitzgerald 1,214 to 429. Although each candidate carried nine counties, Crockett is correct in saying he "had a majority [a plurality]" in 17 counties, if all their votes were combined. Leaving out Madison entirely, the total vote in the other 17 would have given Crockett the victory, 7,519 to 7,320. Since he had lost (in the 18 counties) by the narrow margin of 586 votes out of 16,482 cast, Crockett contested the election, but the House Committee on Elections accepted the official returns and gave Fitzgerald his seat. *Niles' Weekly Register*, XLI, 332; Record Group 233, National Archives.

which was very strong, and which was the county that had given the majority that had beat me in the former race, should be left off from my district.

But when the Legislature met, as I have been informed, and I have no doubt of the fact, Mr. Fitzgerald, my competitor, went up, and informed his friends in that body, that if Madison county was left off, he wouldn't run ; for " that Crockett could beat Jackson himself in those parts, in any way they could fix it."

The liberal Legislature you know, of course, gave him that county ; and it is too clear to admit of dispute, that it was done to make a mash of me. In order to make my district in this way, they had to form the southern district of a string of counties around three sides of mine, or very nearly so. Had my old district been properly divided, it would have made two nice ones, in convenient nice form. But as it is, they are certainly the most unreasonably laid off of any in the state, or perhaps in the nation, or even in the te-total creation.[15]

However, when the election came on, the people of the district, and of Madison county among the rest, seemed disposed to prove to Mr. Fitzgerald and the Jackson Legislature, that they were not to be transferred like hogs, and horses, and cattle

s 2

15. This is an exaggeration. It included the six counties in the northwestern corner of the state and the middle two (Haywood and Madison) of a tier of four south of that group. *Public Acts*, 1832, extra sess., p. 14.

16. In his letter of Jan. 7, 1832, Crockett wrote: ". . . the thing that had the name of beating me— took the Jackson ground against" the national bank. According to a dubious "Reminiscence of Davy Crockett" in *Every Saturday*, XI (Nov. 25, 1871), 515, when Crockett and Fitzgerald (incorrectly named James instead of William) met in Paris, Tenn., during the canvass, Crockett threatened that if Fitzgerald repeated a previously made charge, "he would thrash him." When Fitzgerald did so and Crockett advanced toward him, Fitzgerald suddenly pulled out a pistol and forced Crockett to back away.

17. Adam Huntsman was a lawyer and politician of considerable shrewdness, and a political writer of force. In 1833 he opposed Crockett's candidacy, though not himself running, and wrote a number of tracts calculated to defeat him. Mooney, "Adam Huntsman," 99–126. The tract, "Book of Chronicles, West of Tennessee, and East of the Mississippi rivers," to which Crockett refers was a fine attack on his political motives, written in Biblical language by Huntsman in 1833. It was quoted extensively in *Life and Adventures*, 116–26 (also, *Sketches and Eccentricities*, 129–36). The following brief quotation will indicate its flavor: "I. And it came to pass in those days when Andrew was chief Ruler over the Children of Columbia, that there arose a mighty man in the river country, whose name was David; he belonged to the tribe of Tennessee, which lay upon the border of the Mississippi and over against Kentucky . . . ."

18. His actual margin in 1833 was 173, according to official returns (Crockett, 3,985; Fitzgerald, 3,812). Keating, *Memphis*, I, 179–80 (giving the incorrect date 1831—when he had lost) says Crockett's margin "had been cut down to a perilously close figure by the efforts of Judge Overton," but he says further that Crockett declined to run again in 1833,

in the market; and they determined that I shouldn't be broke down, though I had to carry Jackson, and the enemies of the bank, and the legislative works all at once.[16] I had Mr. Fitzgerald, it is true, for my open competitor, but he was helped along by all his little lawyers again, headed by old Black Hawk, as he is sometimes called, (alias) Adam Huntsman, with all his talents for writing "*Chronicles*," and such like foolish stuff.[17]

But one good thing was, and I must record it, the papers in the district were now beginning to say "fair play a little," and they would publish on both sides of the question. The contest was a warm one, and the battle well-fought; but I gained the day, and the Jackson horse was left a little behind. When the polls were compared, it turned out I had beat Fitz just two hundred and two votes,[18] having made a mash of all their intrigues. After all this, the reader will perceive that I am now here in Congress, this 28th day of January, in the year of our Lord one thousand eight hundred and thirty-four ;[19] and that, what is more agreeable to my feelings as a freeman, I am at liberty to vote as my conscience and judgment dictates to be right, without the yoke of any party on me, or the driver at my heels, with his whip in hand, commanding me to ge-wo-haw, just at his

pleasure.   Look at my arms, you will find no
party hand-cuff on them !   Look at my neck, you
will not find there any collar, with the engraving

> MY DOG.
>
> ANDREW JACKSON.

But you will find me standing up to my rack,
as the people's faithful representative, and the public's most obedient, very humble servant,

DAVID CROCKETT.

THE END.

which is, of course, another error. After his victory
in 1833 he ran again in 1835, but was defeated by
Adam Huntsman, 4,400 to 4,652, according to official returns.

19. Jan. 28, 1834, is probably correct. Crockett
dates his Preface Feb. 1, 1834. On Feb. 3, the manuscript went to the publishers, Carey and Hart.